Rx for Success

Follow your dreams
Love
1997

Eph 3:20

RX for Success

How To Turn Potential Into Unlimited Power

96 Tested Prescriptions Complete with Weekly Action Plans

by
Luella Gunter

Lupresco
ALBUQUERQUE, NEW MEXICO

Printed in the United States of America

Library of Congress Catalog Card Number: 96-95331

International Standard Book Number: 0-9655691-0-1

Cover design by:
Jim Gerrish
DayStar Design
Uvalde, Texas

Book design and typography by:
Business Graphics, Inc.
Albuquerque, New Mexico

Printed by:
Thomson-Shore, Inc.
Dexter, Michigan

Published by:
Lupresco Inc.
Albuquerque, New Mexico

Contents

Attitude Development

Dealing with Apathy

Accepting Responsibility

Ethics

Confidence Builders

Happiness Through Significance

You Can Do It

Introduction and Instruction

Congratulations for reaching out and buying yet another book to help you along your journey in life!

I am sure you are interested in this book for the same reason it has been written: **To help you reach the success in business and in life that you desire and deserve!**

You will find each subject is motivational, but more importantly, you have a guide to keep you on a steady path of business success and self-improvement. Your imagination will be stirred as you read, so be sure to keep a note pad handy to write your thoughts as you progress through each chapter.

Each action plan is simple and well within your ability. **Rx for Success** is designed to be read one chapter at a time, applying the suggested activity at the end of each lesson. When you do this, each one will be ingrained as part of your personality, and growth will follow. The activities tie together and sometimes repeat, so you will find you are forming a work ethic, an attitude pattern and personality traits that blend together to build you into the successful, happy person you desire and are working to become.

Rx Instructions

ONE:

Read each chapter, one subject at a time.

TWO:

Put into practice the suggested activity of that subject until it becomes natural for you.

THREE:

Go to the next subject and repeat instruction one and two.

FOUR:

Using the same procedure as above, complete all the chapters. When you have finished all chapters and have implemented these ideas into your work ethic, personality and attitude, you will find you have made great progress. If you feel you need to review any section of the book, return to it and repeat instructions until you are happy with your performance in that area. Repeating any subject as many times as you feel the need will give you confidence of performance.

FIVE:

Share the book and/or these ideas with someone else.

The message is old, yet new. It is a combination of information I have gleaned from others and put into practice for myself during 22 years of working on a job and another 30 years in direct sales. I truly have tested every one of these messages. I know they work for me and I am confident they will work for you and that you will use them with enthusiasm.

My best regards for your abundant life!

Luella

In Appreciation

For all the many people I have worked with who enriched my life. For the opportunities that were available to me and the training and encouragement that came with opportunity.

To my husband, Pres, who is a constant support, critic and mentor. And to Jamie, my assistant, who keeps me in line and is always available. To Melinda, my friend, who encourages, pushes me and shares ideas with me.

And to you for purchasing this book. Now make it work for you!

Luella

Business Development

Goal Setting

AFFIRMATION:
I am a goal achiever because I have the commitment to follow through with my plan of action with a sense of urgency to meet goal deadlines. By the grace of, God I always achieve the desires of my heart.

MAKE THE DECISION

Without a doubt, the most important step to setting any goal is making a definite decision to obtain the desire of your heart.

Until a decision is made, we are at the mercy of the world around us. We have no plan, no definite finish line, our desires float around in the universe and our thinking does not crystallize. How can we possibly zero in on the desires of our hearts if we have not clearly defined them?

Four major areas of our lives in which we set goals are:

Spiritual ***Personal*** ***Family*** ***Business***

While this book focuses on being successful in business, it is important that goals set for your life are compatible in all four of the above areas.

One area of your life affects another area; everything works together to create the "Whole Person"—you.

When making a decision ask yourself these questions:

"Who am I?"

"Where am I?"

"Why am I here?"

"Where do I go from here?"

"Is my desire spiritually and morally acceptable?"

"Will achieving my goal bring harm or ill will to anyone?"

It is important that you feel comfortable that your goal is acceptable in all areas of your life. Honesty and self-respect are essential for you to have real success in business.

DEFINE YOUR GOAL

Do not concern yourself about being capable of achieving the results—that will come later. Write, in detail, with pen and ink, your "impossible dream." As you write, feel the emotions of having accomplished your desire and what this will mean in your life and in the lives of those you love and are important to you.

 **SUGGESTED ACTIVITY:**

Take a day or one-half day off. Go to a quiet place where you will not be disturbed. Take a pen and a writing pad with you. Concentrate on your desires and write you decision boldly and affirmatively on a sheet from your writing pad. If you have trouble making a decision, draw a line down the center of a sheet of paper. On one side of the line write all the benefits of having made this decision; on the other side write down all the drawbacks of having made this decision. If the positive outweighs the negative and, after completing this exercise you feel good about it deep within your soul (even if you may be a little frightened), you have made the right decision.

THE PLAN

Having made a decision for your goal and having committed yourself to achieving that goal, you will establish a plan which will guide you to achieve the desired results.

You need to know exactly what is required in order to achieve your particular goal. Know the rules. For business-oriented goals, this may be done by studying guidelines from booklets that are available in your particular field and, also, by talking to and confiding in people who have achieved somewhat the same results you are desiring.

Draw from the experience of other people, when possible. Associate with people you feel are successful in the field which you are pursuing. Keep your ears and eyes open and apply every helpful hint that comes your way.

Once you know exactly what activity and achievement is required to reach your goal, write it in very specific terms which you understand. It is very important that you *write* it and do not just read the requirements out of a book. When you write rules or plans on paper they are crystalized in your thinking and you are better able to understand them.

Keep in mind that obstacles will come. If you are aware of this, you will be prepared for the obstacles, and they will not affect the end result.

SUGGESTED ACTIVITY:

Clearly and specifically write your goals on a piece of paper. State exactly what you want to achieve and be specific about the date you intend to accomplish each goal. **This is very important.**

Check to see how working toward your goal will affect you in the four basic areas of life—spiritual, personal, family and business.

Commit your plan, which you have clearly written, to God.

Be sure your health, stamina and general attitude is in tune with your goal. If not, be willing to do what it takes to get it that way. Remember, your confidence and self-esteem will improve as you get into action.

Have a family conference. Inform your family about your decision and ask for their support. Let them know this will benefit them. Help them feel they have a part in your plan.

Review the action necessary to achieve your goals. Outline obstacles that may come and make a plan to overcome them. If at all possible, talk to someone who is qualified, by experience and knowledge, in your field of endeavor and who can give you guidance and support.

THE ACTION

CONGRATULATIONS! You have identified and researched the requirements necessary to reach your goal. Now, the important question is: Are you willing to put forth the effort, the action, the time, the dedication and the persistence to achieve that which you have set out to accomplish? Believe me, it will be worth it to you. Make a commitment to yourself right now that you will pursue your goal and reach it. Life is really worth living when you are working toward achieving a definite goal.

Let's get an action plan:

Look at the total action requirement to achieve your long-term goal. Frightening, isn't it? It is nice that you need not concern yourself just yet with the total action required. All you need to think about is doing the job at hand.

Short term activity:

Break your long-term goal down into short-term activity goals. Now, look at the immediate activity required for the next month. Write it down. Next, write the activity required for each week of the month. From your weekly activity goal, make a weekly plan sheet which will outline your total activities by the week. Refer to the chapter entitled "Time Management Made Easy" in this book to find an example of these forms. You will then break the weekly activity goal down into day-by-day tasks. You have preplanned your work day by day, week by week, month by month, even year by year! You can do anything, one task at a time. Each day, concentrate only on the activity scheduled for that day. Make a daily list of activities necessary and, as you perform these activities, check them off your list. There you have it.

In most self-directed businesses, especially direct sales, usually five definite appointments per week will result in enough activity to make progress. Steady progress and momentum is most important. It is better to have one appointment a day for five days in a row than to have five appointments in one day and do nothing the next four days.

SUGGESTED ACTIVITY:

Using your goal performance requirement sheet, make a definite outline of how many appointments you are going to hold each week until you have reached your goal or redirected your activities.

Go over this plan of action with someone who has accomplished what you are striving to achieve. Ask for guidance based on their experience.

Review your plan with your family and get their support and agreement that they will do everything possible to help you continue this plan of action until you have reached your goal.

The suggestions in this chapter have helped hundreds, even thousands, reach unbelievable goals. I know they can do the same for you. Count on it!

AFFIRMATIONS

Stating affirmations of having achieved your heart's desire are sure to bring about changes in your life. Always state affirmations in positive terms, present tense. Why? Because the subconscious responds best to the positive. For example, if you state your affirmation this way: "I won't procrastinate," the subconscious picks up, "I procrastinate." A better wording is: "I do things now" or, more powerfully stated: "I enjoy doing what it takes to reach my dream right now."

Address yourself by I, me or your first name when stating your affirmations. Your subconscious mind responds to your first name because, as long as you can remember, you have been called by that name. Also, use present tense when stating your affirmations. For example, "(your name), you attract dynamic, enthusiastic people to join you in your prospering business." Do state your affirmations in accordance with goals you have determined to achieve. As you phrase your affirmations, get a clear picture of what you want and imagine your desire as already having been accomplished. Allow yourself to become emotionally involved. Really use your imagination and dream your big dream, getting a clear picture of the end result when you achieve this goal.

Say your affirmations at least twice daily, early in the morning and at night just before you go to bed. Say the affirmations again, many times during the day. I have my affirmations on the sun visor of my car so I can read them when I stop for traffic lights, etc. Affirmations are vitally important to help you reach your goals. Never underestimate their value.

℞ SUGGESTED ACTIVITY:

Write your affirmations using personal terms (your first name or I, me or my in positive terms, present tense, using action words with feeling). Place this list on your bathroom mirror, your sun visor of your car, at your bedside table (for fun, write them on a white pillow case and sleep on it!), on the ceiling above your bed—in big letters—see it the first thing in the morning and the last thing at night.

Using a tape recorder, record your affirmations, speaking slowly and clearly with a lot of emotion. Repeat the affirmations until the tape is filled. Listen to this tape as you are doing other things. To accelerate, purchase a pillow speaker, place it under your pillow and listen to your affirmations as you fall asleep. Suggested affirmations: "I achieve my goals in record time." "I am worthy of all the blessings and good that God bestows upon me." "My time is now." "I am super successful in my business." "I take charge of my thoughts and feelings at all times." "I am dynamic, determined and worthy of all good things that come to me." Also, definite statements reciting your specific goal having been achieved. For example, "Congratulations (your name). It is (state specific date) and *you* have reached your goal to (state specific goal). You are *wonderful*!"

Now, go forth and achieve your goals. Expect to reach them in the time set. If for some reason you do not, do not give up. Just reschedule your plan, setting a new time limit and keep pressing forward.

Notes

Self-Motivation

AFFIRMATION:
I have within me a force that impels me into positive action which brings growth and new direction to me. I know where I am going because I am a self-motivator for positive outcomes in my life.

SEEING THE END RESULT

Possibly the best self-motivator is the ability to dream big dreams and put yourself in the picture, seeing yourself already having accomplished your heart's desire. Meet with positive, capable leaders. Associate with excited, successful people. Attend special workshops and seminars. These are a few activities that can give you outside motivation. Outside motivation does not keep you going in the ups and downs of life, but it prepares and trains you to be a self-motivator.

In order to accomplish what you want in life, you must learn to be a self-motivator. All successful people are self-motivators.

A motive is the urge within an individual which incites action such as an idea, emotional desire or impulse. It is the hope or other force which starts in an attempt to produce specific results.

You are motivated by your main goal in business.

As you see yourself imagining what you will be when you have achieved this ultimate main goal, you get the picture of what you will become when this impossible dream has been accomplished. You are able to claim it as reality and you are self-motivated to make it happen.

 **SUGGESTED ACTIVITY:**

LEARN everything you can about the goal you are pursuing.

Practice actual job performance as often as possible.

Practice visualization of having achieved your goal. Set aside 10 minutes a day to relax and see yourself having achieved your heart's desire.

SEE THE END RESULT...
FEEL THE END RESULT...
MENTALLY RECITE THE END RESULT

Write on a piece of paper how you felt, how you looked and who you were when you had achieved this desire. You may share this with one or two special people who are of like mind as you, or you may keep it private. The conviction you have made is to yourself.

WHAT DOES IT TAKE

Self-motivators are self-promoters. If you are in business for yourself, you must become self-motivated.

When you are working for someone else, others tell you what to do (job description), when to come to work, when to stop work (work hours) and how much to get paid (pay scale for job).

When you are in business for yourself you have no one to tell you what to do, when to work or how much you will be paid. You make these decisions, so be a good taskmaster.

Some traits you can develop which will help you are:

PURPOSE:

Have a definite purpose, set your goals high.

DISCIPLINE:

Be willing to do what is required now. Stop procrastination. Be aware, procrastination is a thief. It steals your time and your dream. It is a liar. It tells you you will do the job at hand, but you continually put it off. Practice a "do it now" mentality.

ENTHUSIASM:

Love what you are doing to such a degree that it is reflected in your personality. Enthusiasm empowers you with the ability to attract the people who need what you have to offer. With enthusiasm, you will genuinely enjoy your work.

DECISIVENESS:

Make decisions quickly and stick to them. Hesitation robs you of spontaneity and keeps you from moving ahead.

IMAGINATION:

Develop the ability to form mental images of things not actually present, but results which you truly believe will come to pass.

HONESTY:

At all times be honest with yourself and others. This gives you freedom to stand for your convictions.

SELF-RELIANCE:

Have confidence in your own abilities. You will find you continue to develop many more characteristics as unexpected opportunities open to you and as you grow toward becoming a self-motivator.

 **SUGGESTED ACTIVITY:**

Review the above characteristics and grade yourself. To what degree do you possess and practice them? How can you develop and/or improve these characteristics? Make a written summary of your findings. Seek out educational material which will help you learn how to develop these traits. Share your findings with someone you respect, admire and feel can be helpful to you. Because self-motivators find a point of accountability helpful, it is important that you find someone with whom you can trust your innermost feelings.

KEEPING SCORE

Possibly the greatest motivator is the habit of keeping score. We learn the art of score keeping as children playing games and develop the desire to be a winner.

The art of competition is a personality trait that will take you far on your self-motivation program. The characteristic that will develop your full potential is the ability to compete with yourself. Other achievers can set an example for you and they can give you a standard for excellence, but if you attempt to compete with others, you are sure to be frustrated. Compete with the most important person in your life—YOURSELF!

Set a standard of performance for yourself. Determine daily activities and expected results. Tabulate your activity and results each day to see how close you are to reaching your weekly results goal. **Every week decide what your activity and outcome will be.**

By daily score keeping, you will be remotivating yourself every day of the week and you will know how you stand. This will keep you pressing forward. You would not enjoy watching or playing any game if scores weren't kept. The same principle applies to the enjoyment of your work as you "play the game."

Each week, as you have met your weekly performance goal, increase it by a percentage. A 10 percent increase every week will create growth.

If you do not reach the weekly performance goal, continue to strive to meet it and do not increase it until you have met it. After about four weeks, if you still have not met the goal, perhaps you have set it too high, so you should lower the performance demand or increase your activity level. Do not continue to miss the mark as this builds a failure syndrome and can be very demotivating. You must "taste the victory" by setting your standards high enough that you must stretch, but low enough that it is within your ability to accomplish. Never be content to stay at one level of accomplishment. Continue to increase as you achieve.

℞ SUGGESTED ACTIVITY:

To insure meeting weekly sales goals, you may find preparing a Weekly Sales Goal Plan, such as the one at the end of this chapter, helpful. You should prepare this plan weekly, in your own handwriting, because writing it is another way you are committing yourself to do it.

Daily, tabulate your activity, listing what you have accomplished week-to-date and what you have left to accomplish before week end.

Be sure this plan causes you to stretch to accomplish more than you did the week before.

HOW TO MEET TARGET DATES

Self-motivators set and meet target dates. They know to be self-motivators they must have a plan of action with a definite finish date.

Achievers usually accomplish 75 percent of the goal set. Keep this in mind when setting goals. Set numbers, dates and times for about 25 percent more than you expect to meet; this will insure meeting your goal on schedule or ahead of schedule. For example, you want sales of $15,000.00 for the month of July. Your goal will be $18,750.00 by July 20.

Project your plan a year in advance. This need not be detailed.

Project your plan a month in advance. This need not be detailed.

Project your plan a week in advance on a weekly plan sheet. This plan should include all activities (personal, family and business) that you are committed to achieve for the specific week. See the chapter on "Time Management Made Easy."

Each night, before you go to bed, using your weekly plan, make a daily plan for the following day.

Set priorities. Make a list dividing your activities into three categories: Things that must get done. Things that should get done. Things that can wait. When you have made this list, relax a moment and imagine all these activities completed. Go to bed with a happy face. The next day, work your list, checking off each activity as it is completed.

You will find you have more time to accomplish all you expect once you have it on a list (this has crystallized your thinking and you can see it is possible). You will be excited and motivated as you accomplish each task because you are working your plan.

SUGGESTED ACTIVITY:

Make a weekly plan similar to the example entitled "Weekly Plan" on page 24. Prepare a daily plan using the example entitled "Daily Plan" on page 25. Make and follow a Weekly Activity Goal Plan using the format on page 15.

Weekly Activity Goal Plan

Name ______________________________ Date ______________________

"I pledge to myself that I do what it takes to meet my weekly sales goal. Every day I tabulate my sales, getting a weekly total of sales to date so I know how close I am to reaching my goal. I tabulate and follow through on the necessary appointments to insure that I see the people necessary and do the work it takes to reach my goal every week."

Sales goal for the week $ ____________ Appointments I will set & hold this week

	Actual Sales Each Day	Total To Date	Appointments Set	Appointments Held
Mon	$	$		
Tues	$	$		
Wed	$	$		
Thur	$	$		
Fri	$	$		
Sat	$	$		

Notes

Time Management Made Easy

AFFIRMATION:
Right now I appreciate and respect time and I know I can make the most of my 24 hours today because I am in control. I take the right steps to create happiness and I do not put off until tomorrow what needs to be done today. I live in the moment and confidently move forward into the adventure of today.

PLAN YOUR TIME ALLOTMENT

Every day, everyone has 24 hours to spend. Your goal will be to spend your 24-hour days so they will produce the best life possible for you and those you love. Planning is essential. You can "while away" the hours and then regret the loss of time. Time is a commodity that cannot be recaptured, therefore, it is essential to plan in advance.

Make and use a weekly plan sheet. Use 8½ x 11 inch paper. Divide it into seven days of the week, and divide each day into three parts—morning, afternoon and evening. At the beginning of each week, take about 30 minutes to project your weekly activities on this sheet, listing all activities you are committed to fulfill at this time. Then list all commitments you expect to perform during the week, including all business, family and personal activities. Whether you are able to follow this plan to the letter is not as important as having made the plan because when you have made the plan you are in control and not the victim of circumstances or at someone else's mercy. You will accomplish more with a plan than you will with no plan.

Once you have made your weekly plan learn to live in day-tight compartments by planning each day the night before. From your weekly plan, make your daily plan. Divide these tasks into three major categories: Things that must be done, things that should be done and things that can wait. Naturally, the things that must be done will have top priority—do them first. Then do the things that should be done and, finally, the things that can wait. You will be surprised how much you will accomplish when you organize in this manner. As you complete each task, check it off. **What a feeling of accomplishment!**

Play games with yourself. Look at the assignment and challenge yourself to complete it in a certain amount of time. Work to finish within the time limit. If you do finish on time, reward yourself! Take a five minute break!

Plan to work at your most productive time. Some people are day people and some are evening people. It is good if you are a daytime person because that allows you to work at normal business hours. If you can't be at your peak performance during normal business hours, schedule work and appointments as close to your peak performance time as possible. Naturally, if you come alive at two o'clock in the morning, you can't expect to call on customers at that time, but you can be creative at that time.

Take time to rest. Most achievers find if they take 15 minute rest breaks once or twice during the day, they get more done. Put some time in your plan to go into deep relaxation or take a "power nap" for at least one 15 minute period of each day (preferably mid-afternoon when the blood sugar has a tendency to go down). You will find rest periods stimulate you to get more from your day.

℞ SUGGESTED ACTIVITY:

Implement these suggestions.

See the example of Weekly/Daily Plan Sheet at the end of this chapter.

WHAT ABOUT THE PAPER WORK

Do you feel you are sometimes buried in paper work? People in direct sales and management especially feel this way because a good salesperson or manager is not interested in paper work. They want to spend time producing business, not misdirecting time pushing papers.

Delegate as much as possible. Hire someone to do any paper work that does not require your personal attention. Often people feel they cannot afford to pay someone else, but once they make the commitment to hire someone they find they are in a position to earn more money and can afford to pay the price. A job is created for someone else and you have time to do what you do best—produce!

Expedite the paper work you cannot delegate. Go through the mail quickly. Have three baskets and a trash sack. As you go through the mail, discard the junk mail and catalogs that do not interest you. Place all important mail in a basket marked ***"urgent things that must be handled now."*** Put everything else in a basket marked ***"things that should be handled."*** Have another basket marked ***"to be filed."*** Place items in this basket that need to be filed but do not need to be handled immediately. Work your "urgent basket" as soon as possible, placing the finished items, receipts, etc., that will need to be filed in the ***"to be filed"*** basket—work the ***"should be handled"*** basket as time allows. I sometimes take mine with me to handle on the plane as I travel or to appointments to work while I'm waiting in reception areas. Items in this basket do not require total attention and can be done at odd times. Accumulate items in the ***"to be filed"*** basket. You will want to handle it once a week, grouping items to be placed in the same file and working efficiently. You may want to train someone to do your filing for you after you have placed items in this basket.

File everything alphabetically. Regardless how many file drawers you use, have only one alphabetical index and file everything according to subject matter. You will have one place to look and things are much easier to find. This would include all the various programs and articles you receive concerning your line of work. As you read a magazine or trade communication, cut out the subjects you want to save. Place them in files labeled according to subject matter. You will acquire a large reference library of program material and it will be easy to find because it is filed alphabetically, by subject.

Build a library of books. There are so many good books on the market and they are extremely helpful. Be able to put your hand on a book in a minute. Place your books on the shelf alphabetized according to subject matter (eliminating the words the, how, etc.). As your library grows, this arrangement will be a very valuable time saver and you can find the book you want immediately. Use the same system for tapes and videos.

These are simple suggestions. That is the point, keep it simple. People waste too much time "organizing" and get nothing else accomplished. You want to produce, be a mover and a shaker, not a paper pushing time taker!

SUGGESTED ACTIVITY:

Implement these suggestions or hire someone to do it for you.

ORGANIZATION

I have known people who have been "getting organized" for 20 years! This is their way of making an excuse for not moving ahead, it is a form of procrastination.

Perfectionists and nonperformers have this fault in common. The perfectionist is never satisfied that everything is in order at all times and the nonperformer just can't get it together.

Stop worrying about being organized. Hire someone to organize your filing, your library and anything else that you can delegate.

Organize as you work. Get in the habit of putting things back in place after you have finished with them, and do your best to have a definite place for all things.

Use baskets or trays to organize "things." Have a basket for "pick ups" around the house. Put everything out of place in that basket and then, working from the basket, put things in their right place.

If the mail is piled up from several days because you were out of town or for any reason, put it in a basket and then sort it into smaller baskets using the three basket principle described earlier in this chapter.

For quick clean ups around the house, have a bucket with a handle and keep an apron with big pockets, rubber gloves, spray bottles of cleaner, a brush, scraper and cleaning cloths. You can breeze through the house to speed clean and keep that freshly cleaned look. Never spend valuable time doing deep cleaning. Hire someone else to do this nonproductive time-consuming job!

Keep all your personal grooming aids in one place, organized for hair, face and body. Think of this area as your private salon and do all your grooming here.

Organize your clothes in groups that coordinate style and/or color. Group hang them by connecting hangers, one hanger hung on the neck of the one above.

Place shoes and purses according to style and color on shelves or in bags so you can make quick selections.

Keep all other clothes, such as underwear, etc., in separate drawers, grouped according to how they are worn.

Don't concern yourself with doing everything to perfection. Have a good idea of the location of items you will need and you will be able to find them quickly.

Accept the fact that things get out of order, especially, in a working office. To help keep your desk orderly, remove as much from the top as possible. Keep the extra tools in a drawer and put the collector items, pictures and figurines on a shelf. From time to time clear the desk, throw away pencils that don't work. Reorganize, spending no more than 15 minutes to pick up. Have a basket nearby in the event you must clear your desk in a hurry. You can put everything in the basket and hide it temporarily so the desk will look orderly for unexpected visitors.

If you can find anything you need in a matter of five to seven minutes, consider yourself organized well enough to get to the productive work that pays the bills and pays your salary!

SUGGESTED ACTIVITY:

Look around your house and your office. What is needed? Hire someone to get you organized and don't spend your time doing it. Once the major organization is complete, spend a few minutes each day staying organized. Throw away or pack everything you are not using.

MAKING THE MOST OF YOUR 24-HOUR DAY

People who are focused on a definite goal use time much differently than people who are drifting with no precise plan or purpose. Have you ever noticed how much more effective you are, how much more you get done on days that are crowded with activities and appointments?

The days with no definite plans are the ones that drag by, and you feel a lack of motivation. You are anxious and worried about yourself. I have seen people who have a 9:00 to 5:00 job, in addition to a direct sales job, as well as a family and some civic work. It seems these people are able to accomplish more activities successfully than people with very few responsibilities.

I find it interesting that occasionally I see a person quit a 9:00 to 5:00 job, giving eight more productive hours than before and, yet, gets less done.

The answer to the dilemma is focus. Be focused with your plan for each week and each day. To utilize time available, one must have definite plans with an intense desire to stay focused and accomplish defined goals each and every day. Diligently refer to your Weekly and Daily Plan Sheets.

Good health is important to making the most of your time. Do not sacrifice the eight hours of your day that should be devoted to relaxation and sleep. This is a form of time embezzlement. You won't go to jail for this crime, but your body can suffer a fate worse than jail by sleep deprivation. People who are focused on a definite goal find it is essential to protect their health at all times. This includes rest, relaxation, mental and physical exercise, proper diet and body hygiene. Never neglect yourself or your body. Develop a consistent plan for good mental, physical, emotional and spiritual health, just as you have developed a plan for success in business.

Family and friends are important. Make time for them. Have family conferences and allow each member of the family to share their feelings, desires and commitments. Plan family activities and give these activities your quality time.

When we consider we have eight hours to work, eight hours to use as we wish and eight hours to rest and sleep, we really do have a lot of time. It is not the amount of time we have that counts, it is how we use it. Balance is important and sometimes seems impossible, but awareness helps you stay focused and enjoy the time you have. Make time for the joy of living. A few hours of pure joy and entertainment can make you more effective during working hours. Minutes cannot be recaptured, they cannot be stockpiled. Time must be spent, so spend it wisely.

℞ SUGGESTED ACTIVITY:

Make a list of activities for your work, self and family during the week. Is your life in balance? If not, determine what you can do to correct the imbalance.

Weekly Plan

"This week I plan and spend my time effectively balanced between spiritual, personal, family and business activities. I enjoy and utilize every one of the 168 hours that are mine!"

Name ______________________ Week of ______________

	Monday	Tuesday	Wednesday	Thursday	Friday	Saturday	Sunday
Morning							
Afternoon							
Evening							

Daily Activity Plan

Name ____

Date ____________________

"Today is mine to spend as I please. I choose to live it with serenity and empowerment as I follow my individual plan."

Things that must be done today ____________________

____

____

____

____

____

Things that should be done today ____________________

____

____

____

____

____

Things that can wait ____________________

____

____

____

____

____

Notes

Activity

AFFIRMATION:
I know that action starts in my mind and controls all levels of my existence: Physical, mental, emotional and spiritual. Right now I pledge that I am willing to make sacrifices to perform the action necessary to reach my heart's desire. Each day, by the Grace of God, I move into constructive action for the good of all concerned.

GETTING STARTED

Surely, you have by now set your long-term and short-term goals. Hopefully, you have made your weekly plan and written your daily list of activities. Now is the time to focus on getting started.

Activity begins in the mind. Controlled thoughts result in controlled actions for great accomplishments. All achievement requires a degree of sacrifice, development of plans and strong resolutions. The higher the thought, the greater the success because it is through the intellect that achievements are manifested. Having a plan with intensity to get started stimulates you and keeps you moving all day.

Let's play a thought game. Have you noticed, if you have a 7:00 AM plane to catch, the urgency with which you get out of bed, shower, dress, grab a bite to eat and get out the door? You function with lightning speed because you have conditioned your mind and your thought patterns to do the necessary actions to meet the time limit. You may even sacrifice a few minutes sleep or eat less than usual, but you make the plane on time.

To help you get started, play the game, "I have a 7:00 AM plane to catch" every morning. Condition your thought patterns to follow a rigid, fast schedule to get going and get to the plane (your office) on time. This is especially helpful if you have your office in your home. Make a pact with yourself not to go into your office until you look and feel like a business person.

Using this technique, you can be up, dress, eat, organize the house, dispatch family and be at your desk or out the door to meet appointments, make contacts or whatever you have planned, by 9:00 AM. Do set definite working hours and be consistent in keeping the hours every day.

Using this technique, you have given yourself a gift of success: A sense of urgency. You're awake, alive and enthusiastic, and you can get started and stay focused on tasks and appointments all day long. You're totally committed, able to give each task your complete attention. You have started in high gear and the world is yours, as you accomplish each activity goal, one after another.

SUGGESTED ACTIVITY:

At the end of each day, schedule early rising for the next day. Lay out your wardrobe for the next day. Make a written schedule of activities you desire to complete and set your alarm for an early rising.

Follow the suggestions in this chapter to get your daily activities completed.

At the end of each day, relax and review to see what you have accomplished and how you feel about your progress.

MOMENTUM

Momentum is the speed with which you are moving ahead, and the faster and more focused you are in this movement, the harder it is to interrupt the action. Speed, energy and enthusiasm builds. Once you get the momentum going, it seems nothing can stop you. Nothing is quite so exhilarating as momentum.

Your imagination is greatly stimulated by previous and present activity. You are focused on your definite purpose. Ideas, plans and hunches will come to you in astonishing ways because momentum creates a magnetism that seems to attract whatever you need at just the right time.

Conversely, once momentum is lost, it is very hard to regain because you must recondition yourself to get back to the action, the mood and the impetus.

Often, we see someone who is working toward an intermediate goal and, through consistency and persistence, they build momentum and achieve the intermediate activity goal in great style. It often appears, once this goal is reached, the individual has a tendency to stop and celebrate, resting on laurels so long that momentum is lost. It is difficult to get the momentum going again because the magic of momentum must be recaptured, taking more time and energy.

Use the following suggestion to avoid loss of momentum and have the exhilarating experience of continuing achievement.

> Concentrate your attention and activity on your current action goal but set another intermediate activity goal, just prior to reaching the current action one. When you do this, you have something to look forward to after you celebrate the victory of reaching the original goal.

With this plan, your entire being becomes aware of your talents and abilities. It adds more momentum to your efforts, inspires enthusiasm and faith as you continue to move ahead with consistency.

SUGGESTED ACTIVITY:

Track your progress on your current action goal. Make plans for your next action goal.

Concentrate on current activities, but be prepared to take the next step. Start thinking as though you have achieved your current goal, but keep progressing with the necessary action.

Compete with yourself and increase momentum as you move ahead.

BURN OUT

We hear about burn out and somehow it seems like a dirty word. Surely, no one wants to admit to burn out, though attitudes such as lack of enthusiasm, loss of momentum, anxiety, inertia, depression may indicate burn out.

Here are a few suggestions to help you avoid burn out:

LOVE FOR YOUR JOB OR PROFESSION

Promotes increased activity, increased curiosity and interest to see how you can expand.

Gives you a desire to explore your job, your talents.

Helps you venture into new areas of the job.

Causes you to reach for a higher level on your career path.

Encourages you to make a change, develop a love for a new phase of the job for self-restoration.

ACTIVITY

Keeps you doing what you need to do, not just what you like to do for success.

Alleviates guilt which causes frustration and leads to anxiety.

Cures anxiety.

Gets results.

VISION

Gives you power to see the picture.

Gets you through tedious, unrewarding activity, giving you the ability to look ahead, seeing the end result.

Vision gives faith for the future and faith gives hope and hope gives excitement to achieve.

 SUGGESTED ACTIVITY:

Prepare a written list of all activities you love at the present job level.

Perform these activities with love and vision.

List activities you will love when you reach the next level of achievement.

Reserve a day to spend as though you had nothing to do, nothing to look forward to. Prepare a written list of everything, every activity, every associate you will no longer have, as a result of having nothing to do.

I promise you'll be glad to get back to the rewards and challenges of work after a "no hope" day.

RESULTS

Activity brings a multitude of results and magnificent satisfaction. Here are just a few:

PRIDE OF ACHIEVEMENT. This has built America. You must never relinquish the desire for the joy of accomplishment. Pride in your work will drive you to activity that is not only satisfying but tireless.

INDEPENDENCE. There is nothing quite so rewarding as the feeling of independence. Knowing you have done the job to the best of your ability and knowing that you can do it again gives you independence. You know you have learned the job through actively pursuing and learning the action it takes to accomplish whatever is necessary for continued success.

SECURITY. Freedom from want or deprivation. You have deposited your activity and the returns are safety! Your plan of action, with continuous activity, will bring you security, stability, steadiness and strength.

EXAMPLE. You are in a position of influence when you are actively pursuing your life work. As an example, you can lead countless others to the same feeling of freedom that you have gained, by showing them the way to pursue whatever activity is necessary to realize their plans and goals.

SELF-RESPECT. Pursuing and accomplishing your goals will do more to build your self-esteem than anything else. There is nothing quite so rewarding as having a job to do and doing it well. Planned activity, not just busy work, will put you in a position not only for self-respect but to gain the respect of others.

HELPING OTHERS. Never underestimate the job of helping others. Having concern for others will make the activity worthwhile and insure your success. People who are dedicated to helping others are estimated to be the top 5 percent of the top 20 percent of the highest paid people in the nation!

SUGGESTED ACTIVITY:

Add to the above list other benefits you have found that result from activity.

Make a list of activities that you are pursuing in your work.

Check your motives. Why do you work?

Busy work may be defined as activities that flit from task to task diverting your attention from your immediate goal. Cut out activity that could be classified as "busy work."

Seize the Opportunity

AFFIRMATION:
I acknowledge I have untapped opportunity deep within and I hereby pledge to develop that opportunity and bring out the best in myself. With God's help, I will let nothing stop me from being the best that I can be.

CREATING YOUR OPPORTUNITY

Sometimes we think of opportunity as an opening to success in the work place or being at the right place at the right time. That may be so, but opportunity really means making the most of **your** God-given talent. Opportunity means being willing to do what is required, to be open to change, to take the risk of failure and much more.

WHO ARE YOU? WHAT IS YOUR DESTINY?

You have within you the ability to create opportunity as you become aware of your personality. You build your own thoughts and mold your personality as you utilize your positive feelings about yourself. This may not come naturally. Most people find they need to put forth a great deal of effort to develop the best that is within them.

Develop determination to become a positive, creative, happy, healthy individual. Live the life of abundance. Explore your God-given talents by mentally supporting yourself and amplifying your creative and imaginary powers. Here is an example of an exercise you will find helpful:

Let's say you are seeking information or need guidance on a specific subject.

> Put forth all the conscious effort you have available to secure this information. After you have exhausted your conscious supply, call on your subconscious or creative mind.
>
> Write a detailed request for this information on a sheet of paper just before retiring.
>
> Go to sleep in a relaxed state of mind. More than likely, around 3:00 AM, you will awaken with the answer.

I have done this many times. It almost always works. Even as I wrote these words for you, I remembered where I had put important papers I had looked for and had not found until this minute.

Stop worrying about what other people think, as long as you are doing the right thing and practicing a positive pattern of life.

Be alive to every idea and "open door" that comes along. Sometimes you must open the door, so look for the handle. Give yourself new challenges, stretch. See if you can go a little further, be a little more daring than you've ever been before. This is **developing** opportunity rather than **waiting** for opportunity.

It has been said, "He who hesitates is lost." Many an opportunity has been lost because an individual waited until the time was right, until they felt capable or felt secure and unafraid, or until someone else gave approval. You will never get all "go" signals at once. Sometimes a decision made in the face of many odds turns out to be the right one. Don't wait to seize the opportunities to grow, to reach out, to accomplish.

DO THE THING. THE RESULTS WILL FOLLOW. It is better to attempt and fail than not attempt at all. As long as you have done your very best each time you try, you will find each attempt promotes growth and is of value. You learn and benefit from mistakes, as well as victories. Eventually, you will develop your full potential and achieve what you are striving to accomplish.

℞ SUGGESTED ACTIVITY:

Reach out to someone you've never met. Show interest, ask questions and get to know the individual.

Perform a task in your job or profession that you have felt unprepared for in the past. If necessary, work this activity step by step, following instructions from a written guide.

Expect a little more from yourself than ever before. Write "night letters" to your creative mind asking for information and guidance as you sleep.

Study your personality. Make a list of personality traits you would like to improve. Seek help through books, tapes, counseling, meditation and prayer to make desired improvements.

Make a list of things you would like to accomplish in life. Research to find necessary steps you need to take and get started on your abundant journey.

Find the necessary books, tapes or counseling that will help you fulfill your desire for self-improvement.

HAVE A SENSE OF PURPOSE

When you have an honorable sense of purpose, no matter how demeaning your work may be, no matter your station in life, you will be a happy person as you realize the joy of fulfilling that sense of purpose.

Your work will become pleasurable, and you will project a personality that will attract people to you. You will be able to help others, you will give them a "lift" by your positive demeanor. Happiness will flow back to you.

Make every effort, every action, an opening for opportunity. How do you know what affect you may have on someone else's life or what affect they may have on yours?

Believe every individual and everything, good or bad, has come to you as an opportunity to help you fulfill your destiny, as you pursue your purpose to serve others, and have an abundant life.

Today I was looking for a coin purse I urgently needed before leaving on a trip. My time was limited and in the hurry I became careless and turned over a basket full of papers. What a mess! How aggravating! But what an opportunity! As I bent to pick up the papers, there was the coin purse. Somehow it had gotten in the basket (where I would never have looked). I tell you this to demonstrate there is opportunity in every adversity as well as in every advantage. It reaffirms my faith in the scripture "In all things, give thanks."

Starting right now, stop worrying about yesterday. Spending time regretting yesterday and worrying about tomorrow robs you of today and stops you in your tracks. Your mind becomes clouded. You lose sight of your goals and negative thinking sets in. Every morning as you awaken, make this affirmation: "Thank you, Lord, for today. With your help, I will live it to the fullest. This is the day which the Lord hath made. I will rejoice and be glad in it."

Sometimes you may feel you are not what you would like to be. This is a natural human feeling which can be dealt with. Accept yourself for the important person you are right now and look ahead to the person you can become. Have a plan for constructive growth with a purpose. Invest in yourself through maintenance. Some people maintain their homes, cars, even their pets, better than they maintain themselves. Look your best outwardly with proper grooming. Feel your best with proper health care. Be your best spiritually. Take time to practice your faith and fellowship with others of the same spiritual belief. Excel mentally through constant feeding of the mind, learning something new every day. Be balanced emotionally with the right attitude. If need be, seek professional counseling.

Check your diet. Are the foods you eat the right foods to give you fuel to charge forth and fulfill your purpose in life? Find the right diet for all areas of your life that will give you stamina and health.

Continue to press forward toward your goals with a plan of action. Do expect to steadily move forward, but keep in mind, you will have setbacks and stops. These are temporary and serve to strengthen you.

In down times, remember your past successes, recalling them so vividly that you feel the emotion of success. This will reinforce your commitment and put you in position to pursue your success plan. Living in the present one day at a time will build your ego and you will feel good about yourself and your abilities. You have resources and determination. Draw on these qualities and exercise your right to success.

 SUGGESTED ACTIVITY:

Challenge yourself. Schedule five to ten more business appointments than you think you can hold and visualize success on each one. Now, go out and fulfill them, one after the other, until you have had a successful finish.

KEEP MOVING AHEAD

Years ago I learned to say to myself "do it now" when I had a job to do or an idea to create. Granted, I do not always "do it now" but often, in retrospect, I wish I had!

Have you ever had an idea for something and then thought, "No, it's too simple" or "Maybe I'll work on that later," and then see that someone else had the same idea and acted on it and it is now a patented, marketable idea? Makes you feel terrible, doesn't it? There is a poem someone wrote that points out all the things she thought of doing but did not and someone else did! Now is the time to keep that from happening to you.

I have always heard, "If a thing is worth doing, it is worth doing right." I know that has merit, but it can hold back the perfectionists of this world. They have a tendency to do nothing until they are sure of themselves. My motto is, "If a thing is worth doing, do it now, to the best of your ability." I had rather make a few mistakes and learn from them than stay in limbo and have regrets later.

Have you ever lost someone you loved and wished you had been more loving while that person was with you? Or, have you ever wished you had acknowledged a person's worth after it was too late? Do you show your appreciation immediately for every act of kindness? Having an awareness and acting on it in things of this nature contribute greatly to seizing the opportunity. In so doing, you become an individual of action who lives in the now and gets things done. You make people feel worthy and you are admired and sought after. Also, you have no regrets.

We learn from reading how to perform job skills; we learn a little more by observing a professional perform the job, but we learn the most by doing the job. Do not wait until you feel you have developed the skill before you start getting experience. It will hold you back and you take the risk of becoming a "professional student" and you never become productive. Unless you are a rocket scientist, brain surgeon or practicing any other life or death skill, go ahead and get started and learn while you earn. This is especially true in direct sales. Once you have the basics and know the presentation and the product line, although each encounter is a little different, you learn to relate to the person to whom you are selling. A vast amount of experience makes you proficient in sales and you find that the more presentations you make the higher your sales efficiency becomes.

Following these guidelines, you will keep moving ahead and your opportunity will become even greater as you become an expert in your field of endeavor.

SUGGESTED ACTIVITY:

Schedule as many sales appointments as your schedule allows. Get moving on each appointment. As you hold these appointments, keep a written memo of the questions you were asked and how you answered. After each encounter, make a written memo on what you feel you learned from that particular encounter. What did you do to increase your knowledge through experience?

Acknowledge with each sales activity (product or opportunity) you are doing "post graduate" work and increasing your skill and education in your chosen field of endeavor. You are, indeed, seizing the opportunity.

RECOGNIZING OPPORTUNITY

Once you have learned that opportunity is within you, you will find that favorable circumstances are everywhere. Starting where you are at this moment, utilize whatever is at hand right now.

Exercise your greatest opportunity which is to build a respectful attitude toward yourself. Such an attitude gives you courage to concentrate on your assets and help you to bring out the *opportunity* within you, which leads to *rich living and great self-respect*.

It is possible to skip over the chance of a lifetime by looking so far into the future, you miss the present. Today is the day of opportunity. The saying "a rolling stone gathers no moss" is true. Granted, change is good, but too much change, or continually thinking the grass is greener in the other pasture, can be a distraction that will blind you to the fortune that is at your fingertips!

Start where you are. Just begin! If you have trouble getting started, think about what you can lose if you wait. Develop a sense of urgency. If you can, make a plan, but do not allow the lack of a plan keep you idle. Sometimes you must start and then the plan develops. Pursuing the opportunity at hand will open your imagination and you will be responding to ideas that seem to come from everywhere and nowhere! Once you begin, you will find one activity or individual leads to another and you are continually moving ahead.

Become known as the person who does a little extra, who goes the extra mile. This will make you indispensable on the job and it will tie customers to you. You will be strengthening your ability to do the job well. People will seek you out of the crowd. You will be in demand. You can take pride in accomplishment and the feeling that you are making a difference in this world. You will learn the secret and reap the reward of seizing the opportunity!

℞ SUGGESTED ACTIVITY:

Write your plan for achievement. Go the extra mile with your plan, yourself and with others.

Always increase the desired number of sales and opportunity appointments by at least 25 percent to guarantee that you will complete the number you really want.

You are becoming a "well-rounded" person. Successful in all four areas of your life—spiritual, personal, family and career! You have so much to give and to gain!

Notes

℞

Just Do It

AFFIRMATION:
Activity generates positive energy and enables and empowers me to realize desired outcomes in my career. I am making my move, reaching for higher aspirations. I have the strength and courage to change things and bring something new and exciting into my life.

JOB DESCRIPTION

It is surprising how many people are not able to give an adequate description of their job or profession. They do not really know what is expected of them or what it takes to excel in their chosen profession.

Make the decision to become an expert in your field. Research your job, your company, your marketing plan and your product.

HOW TO DO THE JOB

Study the words of your sales presentation. Commit them to memory. Find a person who is successful in your field of endeavor. Watch that person make a sales presentation. Practice your sales presentation in front of a mirror. Be aware of your body language and expression. Make a home video of yourself in action, if possible. Finally, learn by experience. Actually go through the sales presentation before you feel you are ready. After five presentations, you'll feel like a "pro."

COMPANY POLICY

Read and commit to memory everything available that describes the company you represent. Be able to answer questions on company policy.

COMPANY PHILOSOPHY

Feel it is "your" company. Know so much about it that you project pride, knowledge and confidence as you represent yourself and your company. Always project accepted company philosophy.

MARKETING PLAN

Know and commit it to memory to enable you to present every step of the plan, from beginning to end. Be so well informed that you can answer questions quickly with confidence and assurance.

PRODUCT

Know and commit to memory everything there is to know about your product. What is in it, how it works and why it works. Be an expert. Do not be overwhelmed. It takes time and practice to perfect your skills.

Being informed gives you everything you need to know for success and enthusiasm for what you are doing. You are enabled to "just do it" in a most extraordinary way!

SUGGESTED ACTIVITY:

Applying the above suggestions, complete your study through reading and researching all printed material.

Meet with at least one individual you feel is outstanding in your business, or a similar business, and ask for opinions and advice on pursuing your career.

Observe at least one outstanding successful person in business making a product and marketing plan presentations.

From your guide or reference material, make a written outline of your company, sales presentation, marketing plan and product information.

PROGRESSION

If you are working on a job or profession that has career progression, then do not hesitate, start right now toward advancement.

Read the rule book or guide that outlines the steps of job progression. Write these steps in detail. When you write something it crystallizes your thinking and you can more firmly grasp the meaning.

Determine where you currently are in your job progression. Referring to the guide, find the next level of advancement available and relative to you from where you are now.

Concentrate on that level of advancement and nothing more. Make a written list of the steps to achieve that level and formulate a plan of action that will outline your required activity to achieve that specific level of progression.

When you have almost reached this level, return to your guide and research the next level available.

Make a written list of the steps required to reach this next level of achievement. While you are finishing the activity to reach the current level you are working to achieve, look ahead to the next level of achievement. You will gain steam to finish the current level and slide right on to the next without losing momentum. You will be repeating this exercise for each step toward each level of achievement on your career path right to the top!

This is called living in activity-tight compartments, taking the tremendous leap to the top, one step at a time. This procedure insures your success and generates enthusiasm for what you are accomplishing. You "build" as you go and you become very strong in the business, learning and completing each step thoroughly as you build a solid foundation.

Achieving the top position in this manner gives you the confidence of achievement. Nothing can undermine your expertise or ability on the job. You know each step so well you can do it over if necessary, but more importantly, you are able to instruct others on the career progression. This makes you a sought after, successful leader and business builder, and gives you the satisfaction of helping others.

℞ SUGGESTED ACTIVITY:

Start your career progression immediately. Refer to the instructions given in this chapter and start doing the research and making your plan for advancement. Write, in detail, where you are now and what you have to do to reach the next level of achievement.

Write a finish date for reaching this next level of achievement. Never underestimate the power of urgency. Set your finish date so close that you will generate a sense of urgency for completion. You will probably complete on target, but even if you do not, you can set another date, but you surely will have accomplished more in less time for having set a close finish date.

SETTING YOUR TEMPO

Your rate of performance or delivery is often in direct relation to the strength of your commitment. Once you have made a commitment to "just do it," you are no longer hesitant, you refuse to draw back and give in to ineffectiveness. Once you are moving ahead, you will find a whole stream of events arise in your favor from all manner of unforeseen incidents, bringing human and material assistance which you never dreamed would have come your way.

The key to success is being focused on the activity, concentrating on the task at hand and doing it in the definite time allotted.

To help you get the most out of your time, you may want to set some daily time limits. Here are some examples which will help you control "time eaters" of which you may not be aware of when you are not focused:

DAILY, SET A TIME LIMIT OF FIVE MINUTES FOR EACH ONE OF THE FOLLOWING ACTIVITIES:

Review your weekly plan sheet and appointment list for the day.

Organize these appointments. Call the person with whom you have the appointment to reconfirm, get travel instructions and give last minute information.

Sort your mail.

DAILY, SET A TIME LIMIT OF 10 MINUTES TO HANDLE EACH OF THESE DETAILS:

Read mail, answer letters.

Touch base with business associates.

Delegate the tasks you can pay someone else to perform.

DAILY, SET A TIME LIMIT OF 15 MINUTES TO HANDLE EACH OF THESE ACTIVITIES:

Read inspirational, motivational material (the Holy Scriptures, self-help book, etc.).

Take a break (power nap, short walk, meditate or "do nothing" time).

DAILY, SET A TIME LIMIT OF 30 MINUTES FOR EACH ONE OF THESE TASKS:

Prepare for meetings that are your responsibility.

Study your guide, journals and work papers relative to your work.

These are just examples and may not necessarily pertain to your particular work, but they give you ideas of how much time to allot for activities. We usually give ourselves a lot more time than is required to achieve satisfactory results. One intense hour accomplishes more than a dreamy, unplanned day. To be in charge of your life, it is necessary to be in charge of your activities. Time moves on, with you or without you. You cannot control time, but you can control your activities and the amount of time you give to each one.

Become aware of what you are doing, how much time you spend doing it and you will have the key to setting your tempo.

℞ SUGGESTED ACTIVITY:

Make a list of your activities for each day this week. Determine how much time you plan to spend on each activity. After completing each activity, check to see if you stayed within your estimated time frame.

Make an ideal plan sheet for each week, listing every activity you have scheduled. At the end of each week, see how closely you were able to stay with the plan. With practice, you will be able to tailor your plan in such a way that you will be working in controlled time frames that will utilize your minutes and hours according to your desire.

MOMENTUM

To reflect on consistent activity, moment by moment, is a successful endeavor. You will find, once you have put your plan into action and have experienced daily energy, everything becomes easier. It is not the consistency of the job that is hard, it is the starting, then stopping and having to start over and over that makes it hard. To build and continue your momentum, outline a definite, continuous plan of action that will be workable and keep your momentum going. Keep in mind, the speed with which you wish to accomplish a given task, or reach a definite upgrade in your career path, will determine the amount of time you will be giving to this plan of action. In other words, if you want to accomplish more in a shorter time, then you will need to spend more hours on your Action Plan.

To keep you interested and to insure that you do not lose momentum, it is important that you schedule a plan of action that consistently has a sense of urgency but not an all-consuming time involvement. Leave some time for yourself and your family.

Making progress and competing with yourself is the most important aspect you will want to consider. This keeps your job interesting and is a self-motivator, empowering you to stay with the program you have set as your plan of action.

THE KEY TO SUCCESS IS: Have a plan of action that is interesting, progressive and not too exhaustive, yet demanding enough to insure progress and success. You will find, as you work your career path, there will be times when you will require more of yourself than other times. This is usually for a short time to help you reach your intermediate action plan in the time you have determined. Having stretched, you can then go back to your normal plan of action for accomplishment.

 **SUGGESTED ACTIVITY:**

Review your plan of action. See that it requires definite activity to achieve the results you expect.

Prepare to follow this plan of action more consistently than before, constantly refining it until you have reached the desired position in your career.

You will be preparing a similar plan of action as you determine your plan to take you to the highest position available or desired.

Constantly seek the next level of achievement. It makes life more exciting and worth living.

Seek help and encouragement from someone who has accomplished what you are attempting to achieve.

Develop a sense of conviction to follow through with your plan. Give it high priority in your life. You will get results and you will be pleased.

Notes

Business Builders

AFFIRMATION:
I am a successful business person because I handle my business in a serious, yet enjoyable, caring way. I delight in service and build a rapport with my customers. I see the big picture, I believe in myself and my company. I am promoting myself to the top of my career opportunity. I am a winner.

WINNING

COMMIT TO WINNING.

Very few people actually make this commitment. Be the exception. Make a contract with yourself for a winning performance!

RAISE YOUR EXPECTATIONS.

People who set high expectations are the big winners. Be a high roller, go for the top. When you set high expectations you are motivated to high performance.

GIVE IT YOUR BEST.

Your personal commitment to high achievement brings out the best in you. Expect a high level of performance. You get what you expect.

KNOW YOUR JOB.

Continue to learn and self-train. In order to learn from experience, you must keep doing the work. With each performance, you get more knowledgeable and you become more efficient, your confidence increases, the work becomes pleasurable as you become more motivated to excel.

STAY HAPPY.

Happiness comes from liking what you do, not just doing what you like. Learn to like every phase of your job.

KEEP REMINDING YOURSELF.

The world is as big as your attitude toward it. You play a very important part as a winner, so stick to your plan. You will find you must have valleys to experience the mountain tops. Your attitude in the valley will get you to the mountain top faster. Soon you will find the valleys are more shallow and the mountain tops higher.

℞ SUGGESTED ACTIVITY:

Each day, stretch higher. Expect to accomplish more than the day before.

Write a letter to yourself outlining winning requirements, your plan of action and how you will keep your commitment to be a big winner.

Share your commitment with one or two other people who will encourage you.

If possible, seek help from someone who is familiar with what you are doing and will encourage you.

Get the habit of expecting a little more of yourself than you feel you can deliver. You'll be surprised at your ability to stretch higher.

REFERRALS

Endorsement of your product by a satisfied user takes away doubt and reluctance and opens the way for you to build new customers. Credible people will speak well for you and refer you to people like themselves.

Value your customer and your association with your customer, not only for reorders, but for referrals. The more successful your customer's experience with you and your product, the more likely you will be getting good referrals.

SOME WAYS TO GET REFERRALS:

GIVE DISCOUNTS.

Offer at least 10 percent credit off customer's purchases for referrals who purchase your product or sign as a business associate. Example: Customer purchases $100.00, gives you a referral who places an order, you owe your customer $10.00 credit off the next order.

OFFER YOUR CUSTOMER 10 PERCENT.

Offer your customer 10 percent of purchases from anyone who is referred to you. Example: A referral buys $100.00, you owe the person who referred the new customer $10.00. This percentage is due from the first appointment and does not include any purchases thereafter.

OFFER THE POINT SYSTEM TO YOUR CUSTOMER.

Example: One point for every referral, each point is worth $1.00 in product, whether you make a sale or not.

If you are not selling a tangible product, then offer a cash bonus or a nice gift for referrals. We tend to overlook the value of referrals. Do not hesitate to ask. If you are rendering the kind of customer service that "ties your customer to you" and if you have established a rapport, your customer will want to share you and your product with friends. Learn to ask for referrals from all satisfied customers every time you talk with them.

℞ SUGGESTED ACTIVITY:

Go through customer files, ask for referrals, offer credit. See how many you can get.

Put a sign on your telephone that reads "**ask for referrals**."

Follow through. Keep track of sales made from these referrals. Inform customers who give referrals that they have earned a credit.

If you attend group meetings, report your results. This will encourage others to do what you are doing.

RAPPORT

Building rapport with your customer and people in general will take you a long way in business and in life. Make a concentrated effort to develop rapport with everyone you meet. You never know how each individual may affect your success and happiness. Good manners, at all times, will insure rapport.

LISTEN TO THE OTHER PERSON'S NAME WHEN YOU ARE INTRODUCED.

Learn the name and remember it by calling that individual by name three times, if possible, at the first meeting. People love the sound of their own name. Using their name in your conversation gets their attention and wins their respect for you.

LISTEN TO OTHERS AS THEY SPEAK.

Often we are so busy thinking about what we are going to say when it comes our turn that we miss the main point of the conversation. Be a part of the conversation. Think of nothing except what the other person is saying. Look the individual in the eye with intensity. Body language, such as nodding, smiling, etc., shows your positive response.

ASK QUESTIONS OF THE PERSON YOU ARE MEETING.

Learn all you can about the interests and desires of the new acquaintance. Avoid talking about yourself and your product before you have done a lot of listening. By listening, you know how to genuinely play to the other person's interests and needs.

MAKE AN EFFORT TO UNDERSTAND THE OTHER PERSON'S VIEWPOINTS AND INTERESTS.

Although they may differ from yours, other people's viewpoints and ideas are valuable to help you build rapport. Avoid discussing personalities, avoid gossip and don't get into arguments. Have an open mind, a live and let live attitude, especially about issues that need not affect your relationship.

BE CREDIBLE, AS GOOD AS YOUR WORD.

Don't promise anything you can't deliver. Always be on time for appointments and promptly send thank you notes and notes of appreciation. If you want to be appreciated, appreciate!

LOOK YOUR BEST AT ALL TIMES.

Dress for the occasion. Use care in grooming. Be stylishly conservative. This is *so* important and often neglected. I will remind you again and again!

SUGGESTED ACTIVITY:

Following the suggestions made here, make a concentrated effort to practice successful rapport-building.

Make an effort to meet five new people each week and practice this method.

Keep a diary of your results. Your diary could become a very interesting book!

THINK BIG

YOU ARE BETTER THAN YOU THINK.

Think about your assets and your accomplishments. Never sell yourself short. Some people feel they are bragging when they admit they are good in business. You are not bragging by stating your abilities so long as what you say is true. Often, you do not have to talk about your abilities. Your actions speak for you, loud and clear.

DO NOT MAKE EXCUSES FOR YOUR SHORTCOMINGS.

Either fix your shortcomings or live with them. Remember, everyone feels a little inadequate at times. It is not wrong to feel inadequate. It is wrong to stay inadequate, if you can do something about it. Inadequate feelings are often overcome by activity.

PRACTICE A POSITIVE MENTAL ATTITUDE.

Use positive words. Use words of praise for other people. Think praise thoughts about others. Avoid trivial things. Focus on positive, good things and avoid getting involved in petty matters. The way you talk and think of others is reflected in your own actions and thoughts and you can become what you think of others. The world is a mirror, it reflects back what you think, how you act and what you say.

CAPTURE THE BIG VISION OF YOUR CAREER OPPORTUNITY.

Really believe what you are doing at this minute is important, and know that you can continue to accomplish more, be more and that you are a part of the "Big Picture." Feel you are making a difference in this world.

GIVE POSITIVE REPLIES.

If someone asks how your business is going, give a big smile and enthusiastically say, "You wouldn't believe. It's all I can handle." That expression fits whether business is good or bad, so you are not telling an untruth, but the way you say it gives the other person the idea it is good. This sets up a success mechanism for you and, first thing you know, your business *will* be *so* good, you wouldn't believe!

KEEP MOVING AHEAD.

You begin to feel inadequate if you stay at one place too long. If you stop learning, you stop growing. Keep reaching for more. Strive for more knowledge, more accomplishment, a higher position. Believe you can promote yourself right to the top of your company career path.

℞ SUGGESTED ACTIVITY:

Make a list of all abilities that you believe you have at the present time.

Make a list of the abilities you admire in someone you know who is considered a success in business. See how many of these abilities you have or believe you can develop.

Look at your career opportunity. Where are you on the career path at this time? How far have you come? What did you do to get this far? Summarize this in writing. You'll find you are better than you think!

As you achieve each step of the career path, you will learn the power of thinking big and you will accomplish uncommon success. You will go to the very top in your company. Believe you can do it and you will!

Notes

℞

The Art of Selling

AFFIRMATION:
I am proud to be in sales. I am successful because I believe selling is the best business available. I know that I can and do render a service to everyone I contact because I have a product, a service and an opportunity in which other people are interested and from which they benefit. I love what I do because I love people.

GAIN THE ATTENTION

Considering the fact that you are selling, you must keep in mind you are not only selling a product, service or an opportunity. First, you must "sell yourself." It is very important that you gain favorable attention from your prospect. You do this in many ways. For example:

THE WAY YOU LOOK. You are a commodity, so package yourself in a manner that will gain favorable attention. People do judge you by the way you look. The clothes you wear, conservative yet stylish, well put together, not intimidating and yet business-like, dressed for the occasion with the look of success. Grooming is vital. It is important to look as though you care about yourself—a good haircut and style that presents a current, acceptable look and that compliments your features. It is important to enhance your looks with proper makeup and skin care subtle enough so that it does not offend and yet applied so it makes a statement of caring about how you look. These seem like small matters, but they are very important to attract the kind of clientele that you want and who will be valuable to you. Fair or not, often people judge your abilities by the way you look. If you drive a car, keep in mind these same principles work with your automobile. No one wants a dirty, beat up wreck parked in front of their house or business. Keep your car, no matter how old it may be, in good, clean condition. It makes a statement for you or against you.

THE WAY YOU ACT. Business-like, yet personable. Enthusiastic but not boisterous. Interested but not overwhelming. Knowledgeable but not condescending. Just be open, genuinely interested, friendly and of good character.

HOW YOU PRESENT YOUR PRODUCT. If you use business cards, be sure they are well done and in good taste. If you use company brochures, be sure they are up-to-date and in good condition. Be discreet in displaying and handing these items to your prospect. Handle them as though they are the most wonderful possessions in the world. To you, they are! Show pride in your product and show an interest in how your product or opportunity will benefit the person with whom you are dealing—the initial approach is your first step to closing the sale. If you have a display, keep it simple and make your arrangement basically from the product you are selling. Focus on the item you most want to sell at this particular appointment and make it the main feature of your display and presentation.

℞ SUGGESTED ACTIVITY:

Check your appearance and your automobile; your business cards and business brochures. See if you are meeting the high standards you, your company and your potential customer expect from you. If you are not, then bring them up to standard. You are building an image for success.

Once you are sure that you meet proper business standards, set a definite time each day to practice gaining favorable attention by making at least ten contacts per day. At each approach, present yourself, your business card and/or business brochure with confidence and interest.

Keep a diary of your results. You will find you improve with time and experience.

GAIN THE INTEREST

Most people are interested in themselves and their needs, desires and wants. It is a part of survival. We are born with a tremendous will to survive. Make people like you by listening to them talk.

ASK QUESTIONS. You do 20 percent of talking, 80 percent of listening with identifying needs. Ask open ended, indirect questions that cannot be answered with yes or no. Example: "Tell me, what does the product you are now using do for you?" or "Where do you expect to be on your present job five years from now?" or "What would it mean to you and your family if you (buy) (do) this?" These questions require answers and give the prospect a chance to talk and gives you the opportunity to know the prospect.

LISTEN. Listen to the tone of voice. Does it sound interested? Enthusiastic? Plaintive? How is the energy level? High energy tends to show interest; low energy depicts low interest or loss of interest. How about pacing of words? Are they thoughtful, and slow or fast and careless? Does the response show interest? Learn to read your prospect. This is almost a science and all people in business learn it from intense interest and experience.

TRULY HAVE YOUR PROSPECT'S INTEREST AT HEART. Show a real desire to demonstrate how your product will fill the needs of others, is best for them and will give them the results they want. Repeat these needs as they are revealed to you by the way your prospect answers questions. Continually ask for reactions, feelings and opinions. If the individual uses words like need or should, then that individual is probably security motivated and you will want to present your product, service or opportunity so that it will give a sense of security and well-being. If the individual uses words like desire or want, then that prospect is probably recognition motivated and you will present your product, service or opportunity so that it will give pleasure, status and recognition. Forget about your needs and always think about what will make your prospect happy. Do not expect your prospect to relate to you. *You* relate to your prospect.

GAIN THE CONFIDENCE OF THE PROSPECT. Explain or demonstrate how your product or opportunity will benefit the individual. This is done by personal observation, by use of testimonials, fact sheets and the actual demonstration. By your enthusiasm, honesty and genuine belief in your product and in your prospect's needs, you will gain their confidence in you and you will be able to create the desire and make your presentation so exciting, so enthusiastic and convincing they will want your product or opportunity with all their heart. The ability to do this is a gift and it can be and is learned with practice. Desire is created by giving hope. Making positive claims and backing them up with action, using positive publications and the positive testimonies of other people's success will instill hope and create desire. Never make false claims. Acquaint yourself so well with your product, opportunity and the positive results from it that you will be able to make a presentation that will incite desire to the degree that your prospects feel they can't live without it!

℞ SUGGESTED ACTIVITY:

Contact ten people each day with the goal of securing an appointment. Ask questions. Listen to answers and get the appointment by convincing them that you will be able to fully inform them about your product, service or opportunity. Concentrate on getting the appointment, not informing them about the product at this time.

Spend time studying your product and opportunity so that you will know everything possible about your presentation and be able to answer questions with knowledge, honesty and enthusiasm.

Keep a diary of your progress.

CLOSING THE SALE

You have gained your prospect's interest, won their confidence and created a desire within them for your product or opportunity. Because your prospect trusts you, you are now ready to sincerely and enthusiastically paint the picture, show and help your customer visualize the end results. Genuinely feel your customer's trust in you to help them make the decision. Close concisely, correctly and comfortably; summarize how the product works, what the product does and why.

MAKE YOUR PRESENTATION WITH FLOURISH. Sincerity and emotionalism sells. Professionalism is important, but use it with ease.

Closing questions are important. Always ask "open ended" questions, ones that cannot be answered with yes or no. Example: "How do you like the way the product feels, looks, works, etc.?" Get a response to this type question. Move ahead with another question—give them a choice. Your prospects want assurance that they are making the right choice. Using two examples, explain the pros and cons of selecting one over the other. Keep the package simple. Specialize in one or two packages. Giving too many options can be confusing and they make no decision. Sell the most important items on the first encounter. Follow up with other items in your line, once the customer relationship is established.

The same thing applies when presenting your opportunity. Help your prospect make the decision before you go into training, inventory and business suggestions.

FINALLY, MAKE STRONG OFFERS AND PRESENT THEM UP FRONT. Show the customers how they can benefit.

GIVE NO MORE THAN TWO OPTIONS. "How would you like to start, this way or that way?" or "Which product do you want to take home now, this one or that one?" Specifically describe these choices.

Once you have given these options, say no more. No matter how long it takes to get the reply, wait with positive expectancy. This is not easy, but knowing it works, you can do it. Usually, if you speak again before your prospect does, you lose the sale, or at least you have to go through the entire procedure—gaining attention, developing interest, gaining confidence and desire, and closing all over again!

Lean in slightly when asking for the order. Look pleasant and be direct. Watch your voice. Use the same tone and firmness you have used during your presentation. Smile, in your voice and in your eyes. Feel positive that you are rendering a service to your customer by closing this sale.

SUGGESTED ACTIVITY:

Practice the art of the sale at least five times with real people, showing them your product, service or opportunity and going through all the steps you have studied in this chapter.

THE REWARDS

More success, achievement and happiness come through strengthening your belief system in yourself by experience in selling. All successful sales people love and believe in the product, service or idea they are selling, as well as the people they are serving. They have the best of all worlds.

Sales people learn how to meet people, get along with people, really enjoy them and earn their trust. People in sales have the opportunity to associate with prosperous, interesting people. They learn from everyone with whom they work, and often make meaningful, valuable relationships that last a lifetime.

Sales people attract prosperity because they become professional, respected individuals, capable of earning unlimited income. They know they are paid in direct proportion to their efforts and they learn to be effective, knowing the more people they serve by making more quality contacts, the greater their income, success and happiness.

You are very fortunate to be in sales! Learn people skills, learn to plan your time and prioritize your time to allow you to help more people. Once you have a plan, stay focused and enthusiastically follow through. Results are sure to come.

℞ SUGGESTED ACTIVITY:

Refer to your daily plan.

How many calls do you plan to make today?

How many sales will you make today?

What is your $ income today?

Each day write the answers to these questions in the form of affirmations:

I am making _____ sales calls today!

From these sales calls I am excited because I am making _____ sales resulting in $__________ income today!

Recite these answers to yourself many times during the day.

EXPAND YOUR BELIEF SYSTEM,
ALWAYS REACH FOR MORE.

PERFORM THE ACTIVITY,
THE RESULTS WILL COME.

YOU CAN HAVE IT.

YOU ARE IN SALES!

Notes

℞

Correcting Career Killers

AFFIRMATION:
I have what it takes to overcome career killers because I am informed, dedicated, committed and have God's blessing on my work.

PROCRASTINATION

Too often we make the mistake of putting off commitment. We say we will get serious about our career a little later making statements such as: When we are older, have more money, when the kids are grown. There are always a multitude of reasons.

When we put off ambition, or when we allow something or someone to hold us back, we exercise the will to fail. Sometimes we use self-denial because we fear failure. You must act now, in this moment, at this age, if you are to fulfill your potential. If you do not, you will look back with regret of years wasted, never to be recaptured.

Sometimes you must be willing to take chances and sacrifice security in order to pursue the work you enjoy and for which you have the talent. If you refuse to take chances, you can hold yourself back for years, endangering your opportunity for outstanding success.

It is not easy to "put everything on the line" and take chances, make sacrifices and work diligently in lean times, but those who do are the ones who experience the glory of fulfillment and they are the leaders in this world. They blaze the trails for others to follow.

Play for the rewards of life! Stop making excuses and taking detours. Instead, give it your all right now! You'll be amazed how much you can accomplish, how much energy you have and how enthusiastic and happy you will become!

How do you break the habit of procrastination? Take small steps. Just start. Do not wait to be inspired, inspiration comes with activity. Great writers and orators say they were not inspired to sit down and write masterpieces, but, once they started, the thoughts came. You may have to force the first few steps, but before you know it, you will be caught up in the joy of achievement and one thing leads to another and you are on your way.

SUGGESTED ACTIVITY:

What have you been intending to do and have not done? Make a written summary of this activity or activities.

What would you like to do but have been afraid to attempt? Make a written description of this activity and list your fears of following through.

Who have you wanted to contact but have hesitated, for one reason or another, to do so? List these names.

You may think of other areas to consider. Regardless of what is causing your procrastination, face it, address it and do what it takes to overcome it. Start acknowledging it by written description. When you see it written it does not seem so impossible and you can handle each item on your list, one at a time. Seeing your written list will motivate you to action and you will do it now, whether you want to or not. You will force getting started. You will finish with great satisfaction for you have started to overcome and master procrastination.

Say, "do it now" out loud to yourself, seven times, three times a day. After 21 days your subconscious will be programmed to keep the body moving and you will not hesitate when it comes time to act because somewhere inside you'll hear a little voice saying, "do it now."

RESTING ON YOUR LAURELS

We see it many times: An individual who starts a project or career and really gives it their best, accomplishing outstanding results, only to fade into the background or fade away altogether. What is wrong? Why should this be?

Possibly, having achieved great results, the individual basks in the "glory of the moment of success" too long, loses momentum and does not have the will to get it back. The feeling may be, "I'll never be able to do it again," and so, with fear of failure, does not have the will to try. Or possibly thinks, "is that all there is?" and is unwilling to venture any further into this journey of success. There are any number of reasons why people rest on their laurels and never accomplish their full potential. We could list reasons to fail forever, but instead, let's explore ways to avoid this tragedy.

To accomplish your full potential, you must have a plan of action to meet the requirements of success. Perhaps one of the most effective plans is the art of competing with yourself. Always expecting more of yourself makes good sense. How do you think records are broken? Not by competing with the record the other fellow has set, but by competing with yourself to the point that you become so good that you break the other person's record! It is your own record that you need to watch.

Granted, life goes in cycles. We have peaks and valleys, but need our peaks be so high and our valleys be so low as to defeat us? Not if we have a plan. Recently, I was counseling an individual whose team, in order to qualify for a reward, had to accomplish more than ever before. She said, "But we've never done that much." My reply was, "Sooner or later you are going to have to do more than you have ever done before or you will never break the barrier!"

We must not compare what we have done with what we are going to do. Rather, we must use what we have done as a springboard to do more. Always increase. If you are in sales, look at your sales for this week. Now, set your sales goal for next week 10 percent higher. Keep your eye and your heart on that goal. Each week continue to increase by just a bit. Do you want to start getting up an hour earlier every morning? Start by getting up 15 minutes earlier each day for three days, then move it to 30 minutes, etc. In two weeks, you will have acclimated yourself to get up an hour earlier.

It does not take much to break the habit of resting on your laurels, if you will continue to increase a little at a time. And it makes the game of life so exciting! Sometimes, we expect too much too soon, and the end result is nothing. Take it a little at a time. When you reach a goal, bask in the glory of the moment for that long, a moment. Look ahead to what you are going to accomplish next. Doing this, you will have overcome the career killer of resting on your laurels.

SUGGESTED ACTIVITY:

Increase your sales record by 10 percent over last week. Make five more contacts this week than you made last week. Select any area of your life you wish to improve, and set about to do it, using the principle of small increases.

Use the affirmation: "I continue to break my best record and I enjoy competing with myself. Each day, by the grace of God, I do better and better."

Old Chinese Proverb:
"He who rests too long on his laurels is always on the bottom."

SUPERIORITY

This is a serious career killer, completely unnecessary, yet, we see it time after time. There are many reasons for a superior attitude. One reason being a cover up for feelings of inadequacy or to hide intimidation. Correcting this is not easy, but can be done by forgetting yourself and concentrating on others. Reach out to them and allow your ego to take the "hard knocks." You will find this is wonderful therapy because it builds self-esteem and your success will outweigh failure.

Sometimes an individual who accomplishes a degree of success suddenly feels "too good" to continue to do the activity that created the success. This results in skidding and spiraling down into failure and despair, and the individual wonders why. The cure for this would be to keep your eyes on more activity to generate more success, and never feel too proud to do what it takes to continue to move ahead.

Some people are simply trapped in this "air of superiority" personality complex. They have embraced certain prejudices and preconceived ideas for so long that they are not aware of their attitude. It is never too late to change. Often this personality fault is due to lack of knowledge about people and lack of experience. If you find yourself continuously passing judgment, get informed about the subject matter. Walk in the other person's shoes. It will give you better understanding and temper the superiority attitude.

Without knowing it, some people have a spirit of condescension. They feel more important than the people with whom they are working, so they descend from their "throne," projecting an attitude of patronizing behavior toward the "little people." Those with whom they work recognize this air of superiority immediately and feel resentful. This attitude can be avoided by respecting others. If indeed, your position is superior to another individual, it is your responsibility to do your job and recognize the value of another human being with respect and consideration. The more important you are, the greater your opportunity to serve others, make them feel important and win their respect.

No matter how high your position or how much you have achieved, if you would be great, be of service. It seems the more important people are (who are **really** important), the more humble they appear and the more willing they are to be understanding and to be of service to others.

You are, or you are becoming, a leader in your field. Lead people by example in the way you want them to go, projecting an attitude of respect they can admire and emulate.

℞ SUGGESTED ACTIVITY:

Call your customers and go the extra mile in service. Think of ways and means that you can give them a feeling of well-being and respect.

Make five sales presentations. Monitor your presentation. Is it mechanical? Are you patronizing the people? Are you showing respect for their feelings?

How do you really feel toward your coworkers? Find a characteristic that you can admire in each one of them. Let them know it. Pay genuine compliments. When you are important in their eyes, you are truly important.

Relax! Have fun! You can't act superior and have fun at the same time!

LACK OF FOCUS

Have you ever felt you were going six directions at once? No doubt, everyone does at some time or another. When you have this feeling, it is your signal to stop short in your tracks, regroup and remind yourself just what you plan to accomplish.

Ask these questions:

What is my ultimate goal?
How will this activity contribute to it?
Is this activity timely?

Answer these questions:

Is it something that must be done now?
Can it wait?

Concentrate on doing the things that must be done now to move toward your ultimate achievement. Prepare a list of your most important things to do each day.

Highly creative people have a hard time staying focused. They get sidetracked and lose their focus, in order to pursue a new idea that may not closely relate to their ultimate achievement goal. If you have this problem, learn, to stay highly focused, you must not allow yourself this luxury of creative diversion. Use only what you need at the time, you may even utilize and carry out other people's successful ideas to achieve the end result.

People who are focused are willing to "pay the price." A lot goes into the plan from the time a decision is made to achieve the ultimate result until the final victory. Some work to get there is more pleasant than other work. When you are focused, you take this into consideration and you are willing to do what it takes to finish successfully.

I once knew a young man who had a wonderful opportunity to work with a famous horse podiatrist. The plan was that the young man would work with the doctor on his horse farm, learn from experience, while attending a noted university, all at the doctor's expense and then, ultimately, the business of this famous doctor would be passed along to the young man. This seemed like a wonderful opportunity. The young man lasted on this plan a total of two weeks and abandoned it. He came home with a different goal which, incidently, he pursued with great success. When I asked him why he did not pursue what seemed to be an opportunity of a lifetime, he said, "Well, all I have done the past two weeks is shovel horse manure." The moral of the story is that the young man did not want the ultimate opportunity enough to stay focused and do what was necessary to reach the end result. Also, the lesson is: To reach your ultimate goal, you may have to "shovel a little manure." Focus on the results. This will give you the incentive to keep on shoveling.

SUGGESTED ACTIVITY:

Review your plan for achieving your ultimate desire.

Review requirements to fulfill this plan.

List the activities that must be done to accomplish your plan daily, weekly, monthly.

Work in day-tight compartments so that you will be able to stick to these activities, even when it becomes difficult to do what is necessary, allowing nothing to divert you from reaching the end result each day. Keep in mind, you can do anything one day at a time.

Yes, you will have times when you can't avoid being diverted, but get back to the activities at hand as quickly as possible. Stay focused by concentrating on the successful end result.

Notes

Visualize Your Future

AFFIRMATION:
I believe in progress. I believe in growth. Day by day I am increasing my level of competence because I am filling the vacuum I have established by extending my desire. Through visualization, which leads to action, I am becoming the person I want to be. By the grace of God, I have the power and strength to achieve the growth I desire.

RAISING YOUR COMPETENCE LEVEL THROUGH VISUALIZATION

An observation, known as the Peter Principle, made by educator Laurence J. Peter states, "In a hierarchy every employee tends to rise to the level of his incompetence." This may be true of some individuals, but that does not mean that you have to settle for less than **YOU** desire.

You have within you the power to raise your level of competence through the use of desire, imagination, need, inspiration, and achievement. As you do this, you will push your level of incompetence higher.

When you have a dream or desire for more, you create a vacuum. Once a vacuum has been established, it must be filled. You will fill many small vacuums, as you raise your level of competence. Increasing competence raises the level of incompetence.

> Example: Perhaps you want the highest position in your chosen field. Where are you now? That is your present level of competence. Each step you take toward reaching the highest position will raise your level of competence.

To raise your competence level, you must focus on precise, clear, definite images of that which you desire. You must practice the elimination of any negative thoughts concerning your ability to reach your desire, shutting out all interference.

To concentrate your thoughts on your entire creative facilities, you must develop a passion and complete dedication to reach your desire. You will find **visualization** gives you the single-mindedness and concentration which will create an atmosphere that will help you move ahead toward your desire, as your creative mind steers you in the direction you wish to go and moves your body into action.

Using the power of visualization, strengthened by positive affirmations, you will be able to image or picture in your mind what you want the outcome to be. As you get a true picture of what you want, you will act accordingly and you will raise your level of competence.

As you work this plan, you will be continually moving forward from one level of competence to the next. You are an achiever and achievers are never satisfied; they continually move ahead.

℞ SUGGESTED ACTIVITY:

Determine your level of competence. Where are you right now in your career? Make a written review of your findings.

Looking ahead to raising your level of competence, determine the next step and write an outline which helps you.

Study, experience and analyze the action steps you must take to reach this next level of competence.

PRINCIPLE OF VISUALIZATION

You have the ability to choose exactly what you want. With your conscious mind, you can visualize performing the necessary steps to achieve and completely map out your plan. You can see the definite objective and yourself achieving it. In other words, you can visualize yourself performing the necessary activity required and you can set definite finish dates. In so doing, your conscious mind notifies your creative mind of your intentions and, as you progress with the plan, your creative mind dictates, guides, creates and inspires.

Your creative mind responds to your imagination and feelings. It believes every thought, emotion and image you put into it, and eventually will reproduce outwardly what goes in, to whatever extent you program it. The following are ways that you program:

REPETITION: Positive action will come through positive affirmations. It is important to repeat affirmations many times each day. Affirmations are more effective when repeated first thing in the morning and last thing at night.

EMOTION: Strong emotion helps the creative mind move the body into action. When stating your affirmations, it is important that you "*feel*" the emotion of having already achieved what you are affirming. Practicing this method will help you act like the successful person you want to become.

IMAGES: As the eye sees, the mind believes. Charts with pictures of that which you desire are very effective because they make your imaging seem more tangible. This increases your desire to do what is necessary for your projected outcome.

Consistent repetition of these exercises should program your creative mind to reproduce as outer reality all that you truly desire.

℞ SUGGESTED ACTIVITY:

Re-identify your desire (goal). Refer to the exercises you completed in the Goal Setting Chapter.

Review why you desire this goal.

Pretend you have already achieved your desired goal. Write a short summary describing the feelings you had as you did this exercise.

STRENGTHENING COMMITMENT THROUGH VISUALIZATION

Having defined your desire and the end result, you established an atmosphere of creativity inspired by your desire, dream, need, opportunity and inspiration. Your creative mind will work for you and motivate you only to the degree of your commitment for the desired result. You can strengthen your commitment as you give your creative mind instructions through positive affirmations and visualization.

As you feed your desire into your creative mind with constant repetition, stated with feeling and the ability to "see" these affirmations, you will be freeing the creative mind to take over and draw on your vast store of personal experience, knowledge, memory. You will also do what is necessary to attract to yourself the knowledge and experience of others. Once your image is clear, the achievement is just a matter of time, persistence and dedication. It seems like magic, but it really is not, it is just the way the mind works!

As you work this program, be sure to be aware of the fact that when you get an idea, desire, inspiration or "hunch," your conscious mind is carrying out instructions that your creative mind has given. It is important that you take action to implement these ideas that come to you in order to facilitate your progress. Be aware and don't be hesitant to act on your inspirations. You will find you are more energetic, more enthusiastic and have a keener mind than ever before because you are "tuned in" to ideas from your creative mind.

Always acknowledge God as your higher power as you are releasing unexplored powers of your mind through imaging. Give credit where credit is due. Your strength must come from a higher source outside yourself, and God is unlimited, so take Him as your partner. Call on Him always, praise Him often and trust Him explicitly. Through faith, confidence comes.

 **SUGGESTED ACTIVITY:**

To prepare yourself for writing your affirmations and for making your chart, do the following exercise:

Make a written list of all the reasons why you have not, feel you cannot or will not reach your desire.

List all your fears concerning reaching your desire.

What are your shortcomings? Put them in writing.

Do not analyze these answers. Set them aside to use later.

VISUALIZATION THROUGH AFFIRMATIONS

To help you get a picture in your mind of what you want to become or what you want to achieve, you will implement your creative mind. To do this, you will find positive affirmations are necessary.

EFFECTIVE AFFIRMATIONS are written with vivid figures of speech conveying mental pictures. They must be written by you and not someone else.

EFFECTIVE AFFIRMATIONS are written in first person using the words I, me, my or, preferably, your first name.

EFFECTIVE AFFIRMATIONS are written in present tense. Prefacing them with the words "right now" or stating a future date in present tense is essential.

EFFECTIVE AFFIRMATIONS are positive, stating what you want, not stating what you do not want. What you are moving toward, not away from.

> *Example:* "I do not eat fattening food" is incorrect. "I enjoy eating healthy, nonfattening food" is correct.

EFFECTIVE AFFIRMATIONS are short and to the point, phrased as if the desire is already accomplished.

EFFECTIVE AFFIRMATIONS use action words and words with feeling. They project a future success that requires stretching, stated in present tense.

Example: "Right now, (your name) you are the magnetic, highly energetic, healthy person God created you to be."

Affirmations get you emotionally involved. Often, your affirmations will be statements totally contrary to what you are and who you are at the moment, but they are designed to project the person you want to become. As you recite your affirmations, you will eventually be able to see and feel like this person you are affirming. In the beginning, you may not be able to get this feeling, but continued repetition will soon convince you.

SUGGESTED ACTIVITY:

Look at your list of inadequacies. Refer to "Strengthening Commitment through Visualization" on page 76. Taking the list you prepared from the suggested activity, turn all the negative personality traits into positive affirmations and write each one separately on 3x5 index cards. The more you write an affirmation, the more indelible it becomes to your creative mind. Post these cards in places that you see frequently. Be sure to put one on your dressing table mirror, one on the sun visor of your car (flip it down at traffic lights and read).

Make a cassette tape of your voice stating your affirmations. Each morning, listen to this tape as you perform your daily grooming. At night, using your cassette player connected to a pillow speaker, listen to this tape as you fall asleep.

Prepare a personalized goal chart. See the following page for instructions.

INSTRUCTIONS FOR MAKING YOUR GOAL CHART

Use an 8½ x11 inch paper.

In the center of the paper, print your name and place your picture. This chart concerns you and must be personalized in this manner.

Just below your name and pictures, in the center of the chart, place a picture or scripture verse that signifies God as your higher power. You are acknowledging that you cannot achieve your goal without divine guidance.

In the upper right hand corner, place a picture that you have cut from a magazine or trade journal which signifies the career position you desire as your long-term goal. Cut out a small photo head shot of yourself and glue it on the head of the person in this picture who projects the success you desire. (This becomes you in the future so choose a good body!) Below this, write the date you expect to achieve this long-term goal.

In the lower right hand corner, find a picture that represents you and/or your family and you, participating in an activity that is a result of your success to reaching your long-term goal. (A vacation place, a material possession, savings account, college tuition, etc.) Paste a small photo of yourself representing you and the other people involved.

In the upper left hand corner, place a picture from a magazine or trade journal that signifies the action that is necessary for you to perform to reach your long-term goal. Paste your head shot in this picture to signify you doing this activity.

In the lower left hand corner, place a picture from a magazine or trade journal that signifies the continued growth from having reached this goal, or the people on your team, or the people in your employ. Put your head shot in this picture to signify that you are in charge.

At the bottom of this picture, write a positive affirmation which motivates you.

Refer to the chart diagram on the following page to give you an outline for this goal chart.

This is a suggested visual aid. You may wish to use this or some other device that is helpful.

Goal Chart

Picture of you performing activity necessary to achieve your business goal.	Picture representing you when you have achieved your long term goal.

Picture of you.

Your name.

Picture or scripture verse which represents your strength to achieve.

Picture which represents success for you.	Picture of you & your loved ones enjoying the results of your success.

Your positive affirmation here.

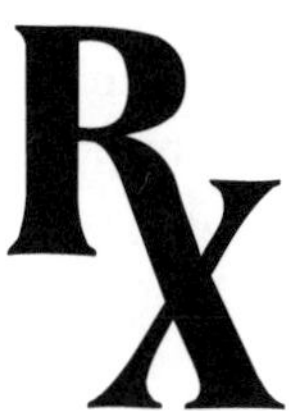

The Importance of Team Work

AFFIRMATION:
I believe that I am on the best team in the business.
I know that winners attract winners and we are the best.
We are growing, individually and as a team,
because we pull together, encourage each other
and love what we are doing.

COOPERATION

Being part of a team is a real advantage. As a team member, you share commitment to a definite purpose and, through this common goal, you benefit from the enthusiasm, imagination and knowledge that is generated in the group.

The spirit of cooperation, sharing of ideas and setting examples for others contributes to your growth, gives you a feeling of pride and a sense of belonging.

Through team work and a spirit of cooperation, you will find your confidence grows as a team member. You will be willing to attempt tasks and work that you would not do if you were on your own.

We all like our "moment of glory" and we are each willing to do a little bit extra to be recognized, praised and rewarded in front of our team. Having a spirit of responsibility to your team gives you a feeling of importance and feeds your ego, building your self-esteem, resulting in your personal growth.

Your personal growth flourishes when you cooperate with the leader of the team, the person who is leading the meeting or the individual who is head of the committee because you feel supportive. When you are supportive, you gain more than you give.

Concentrated team effort toward a common goal builds individuals to their high potential, brings out their hidden abilities and generates energy and ideas as the group goal is achieved.

As a team player, you will find success and happiness because you will cooperate and get excited. You will become genuinely interested in other people, take a supporting role and share in the successful outcome.

SUGGESTED ACTIVITY:

Review your past meeting participation. Do you have perfect attendance? Do you sit up front and support your leader? Are you willing to accept delegation of duties and responsibility? Do you support and encourage your team members?

If your answers are yes, keep it up! If your answers are no, go to the leader of your group and seek help to correct your attitude and to get the spirit of cooperation. You know what to do. For the sake of your success, do it!

TOLERANCE

Effective team members find tolerance a major factor in getting along with others and making friends. Tolerance sparks the imagination and encourages self-discipline and leads to correct thinking, mental growth, knowledge and understanding. ***Never be so tolerant that you sacrifice your beliefs to please others.***

An open mind examines new ideas and new information. It will enhance your ability to grasp opportunity and to reach out to others who look, act and are different from you. Knowing many people from different walks of life will educate you and cultivate your understanding. People are usually intolerant of people, issues and things which they do not understand because they have not allowed themselves exposure to these factors. As a team member, be prepared to learn about others on your team to enable you to accept them for what they are, and to free you from fault-finding. You then have a better opportunity to expose them to your beliefs.

If you are a member of a group and you find you are not getting along with the group or that you are not in agreement, ask yourself why. Have you given yourself exposure to their views, reasoning and background? Fully educate yourself to help you understand the group. The longer you hesitate to do this, the more it threatens your success. ***You do not have to embrace the beliefs of others, but it helps to understand why they believe the way they do.*** Knowing this, you can accept them, even if you cannot accept their beliefs. Tolerance will help you concentrate on the areas in which you agree with others, rather than dwelling on disagreement. You will become more flexible as you find team players may not always agree, but they respect each other's strengths and weaknesses.

As a strong team member, you will develop capacity to endure pain and hardship. You will develop sympathy and forbearance for beliefs or practices differing from, or conflicting with, your own, so long as this does not radically differ from the philosophy of your company or team. Look at every conflict as part of your growth and education in your career. Handle it, grow from it and go forward wiser for the experience.

Through understanding, teams have been known to thrive and grow when subjected to an unfavorable environment. Each team member takes the responsibility for overcoming. The end result is successful team members and a winning team.

℞ SUGGESTED ACTIVITY:

How tolerant are you? Seriously grade yourself on the way you react to people with different beliefs, different backgrounds, different nationalities than you, while taking a firm stand for what you believe.

Make five definite presentations for your product, service or opportunity. During these presentations, be aware of your level of tolerance. After the presentations, make notes of your feelings. Did you have better results from presentations with the most tolerance? Chances are you did.

There are some areas in which you cannot be tolerant. Stand firm. People will respect you if you are not swayed in your freedom of belief.

LOYALTY

Loyalty is faithful allegiance to your team, your company, your cause. Loyalty builds you as an individual. Standing for the ideals and the philosophy of your company breeds respect from others and increases your self-worth. A loyal person is trusted and looked up to by others. Loyalty gives you credibility and integrity.

As a team member, there will be times when you may find yourself in the midst of a "gripe session"—possibly a situation where there is fault-finding with your leader, your team or your company. Keep in mind, such a session can be very destructive to your success because it affects your attitude.

If you find yourself in such a situation, you have the power to turn this around into something positive. Think of the positive aspect of the situation or of the reasoning behind a decision or situation, and point out the good that can result. Or, change the subject altogether. Just as one dissenter can be destructive and tear down the team, one loyal member can build the team.

What if you or the team has a valid gripe? In that case, instead of spending time and energy tearing down your attitudes, settle the issue. Take the situation immediately to someone who can do something about it. Once you have done this, think of the positive aspects of the situation and get on about your business. Some things cannot be changed. Learn to change the things that can be changed, accept those that can't be changed and make the best of the situation. Stop dwelling on negative factors.

If you are associated with a company or a group, one of the most important aspects of your success is loyalty to that entity. Your success depends on it because you cannot project the positive, successful attitude necessary to reach your goals if you are not loyal. Disloyalty eats away at your confidence, your energy and, in time, it will destroy you. You cannot be double minded, you are either for or against your company and your team. Do whatever is necessary to be for it or leave it.

You will find, with enthusiastic loyalty for your company, your team, your job and your goals, you will be filled with the energy and strength to accomplish your goals. Your self-esteem will build and you will help others build. You will make a difference.

SUGGESTED ACTIVITY:

Make a list of all the good philosophies of your team and your company.

Write a letter of appreciation to your leader and pledge your support for any current projects of your team.

Consistently show your loyalty and build your business.

SPIRIT

What is team spirit? We have studied the spirit of cooperation, the spirit of tolerance and the spirit of loyalty, but how do we really put life into these words, topics or attitudes?

Spirit is deep-seated. It is universal and it can be animated, full of hope, love and appreciation. It can also be quenched and full of doubt, disbelief and hatred.

To give life to your spirit, get involved with a group that is full of energy, animation and courage. You will find your own spirit mirrors that of the group because when you are around people of positive nature, you assume the same nature. The reverse is true, so avoid all groups that are negative and resistant to progress.

Be a vital principle of your group and you will benefit from this beautiful spirit of growth, togetherness and happiness. Take part in the activities. Be responsible. Be the person everyone can look to with confidence.

Lend a prevailing tone of optimism and enthusiasm to the group. Something as simple and easy as a warm smile can change the spirit of the entire group to positive expectancy and get successful results.

Develop within yourself a quiet spirit of enthusiastic faith. Believe in the product or service that you sell. Believe in the opportunity you present to others. Have faith that this is the right thing for you and for them. With faith that God is in charge and you are an instrument working through Him, you will be animated when you present your product or service. When you are with your team, your faith will give an added dimension to your personality and radiate the room with quiet enthusiasm and love for the group and the cause.

Positive team spirit is a wonderful attribute and essential to the success of every member of the team. This spirit is generated by each individual member. The strength of the team is made up of members with singleness of purpose: A strong, winning, enthusiastic, positive spirit!

℞ SUGGESTED ACTIVITY:

Review your contribution to the team spirit. Is it positive? If not, take steps to correct this attitude.

Make five sales and opportunity presentations following the suggestion of projecting enthusiastic faith. Monitor your attitude and results.

Share these ideas and your results with your team.

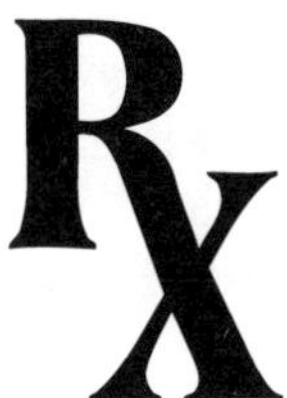

Going the Extra Mile

AFFIRMATION:
I resolve to practice the art of going the extra mile.
I will do more than expected at every opportunity.
This will give me that slight edge that makes a
difference in winning or losing, success or failure,
and it will help me fall in love with my work.

DEFINING THE EXTRA MILE

Just what is "***going the extra mile***?" Is it practiced by our generation? Have we become so sophisticated that we do not think about the little extras? Let's hope not! Doing more than is required, more than is due, beyond expectations, sets you apart, makes you special.

Adding a little extra flourish to delivery, whether it is an assignment, a written article, a speech or product delivery, will greatly impress the receiver, and you will not soon be forgotten! They will call on you again and recommend you to others. It is amazing how people remember the "***little extra things***" you do. Being a little nicer than expected can change your life as well as the lives you touch.

A little bit extra is a very small gesture or service, but it gives that slight edge that means the difference between being the best or being average. Exercise your privilege to perform, to be different. You will receive strong returns for your work, if nothing more than increased self-esteem.

Do something with no expectation for return. You will find the returns do come, and in very beautiful ways.

Let your customers feel they are getting more than they pay for and they will return to you again and again.

To become indispensable in this age of limited service, give a little more than expected; you will be in demand and sought after by the masses.

Put yourself in the position to be paid for more than you do, to be appreciated, to advance and to love what you are doing!

SUGGESTED ACTIVITY:

Review the past week. What did you do beyond the expected? How do you feel about it?

Plan next week: What can you do beyond other's expectations?

Make a list of these activities and pursue them during the week.

Tabulate the results achieved and how you felt about doing a little extra. Did the week go better for having gone the extra mile?

If you attend a group meeting, you may want to share your results.

WAYS TO GO THE EXTRA MILE

In this age of job specialization where one is governed by the job description and paid according to scale, it becomes tempting to do "just what is required" and it seems to make no difference in the respect or pay you receive.

It does make a difference! You may not realize it at the time, but there is a law of returns, and the individual who does a little more than required, sooner or later, is rewarded by this extra effort. You may think no one notices, but someone, somewhere does.

Certainly *you* will benefit by knowing you are giving a little more than is required, that you are doing your best and then some. Your self-esteem will improve, your personality will reflect interest and you will feel part of the company for whom and with whom you work.

If you are fortunate enough to be in direct sales, then going the extra mile will pay direct dividends! You will often see immediate results by putting a little more into your presentation, by giving a little better service.

I used to hold skin care classes. My class attendance and future classes scheduled depended, largely, on the hostess who had invited her friends to share the appointment time. I made it a practice to go overboard for my hostess. I showered her with appreciation and gifts. I had a choice, I could invest in my hostess and future business or I could show greater profit and pay more income tax. I chose to invest in my hostess, which in the long run generated more business, hence, greater profit. She was always presented a nice gift before the class started, before anyone bought anything and, after the class, she was given a gift or percentage of the purchases. I went the extra mile for her many times with the result that I never wanted for additional classes. I felt the way I treated my hostess impressed my guests and inspired them to be hostesses. I was building my business using the extra mile theory. I scheduled classes from classes.

Since I was selling a consumable product, I had reorders. I made deliveries at the planned time. I packaged the order wrapped in tissue paper in a nice bag. I never delivered a reorder without putting a gift in the bag. Maybe it was just a small sample of a new item, sometimes it was an obsolete, but good, item from my product line. My customers always looked for the gift before they checked the order and they were appreciative. They would not think of calling anyone else for product. They were never hesitant to recommend me to their friends.

Have you ever felt strained in a situation but you reached out, in a very small way, using the extra mile principle by just a smile? You never know how much difference a simple smile can make. It is such a small gesture and, yet, such a magical thing with blessings untold.

As you practice the art of going the extra mile, you will find it enhances your personality and you will be known as the individual who stands out in the crowd.

℞ SUGGESTED ACTIVITY:

How many ways can you put the extra mile principle into practice? Schedule at least five sales appointments and implement the extra mile with rewards and appreciation.

Each time you encounter a customer, practice going the extra mile to some extent. Watch the reaction. Chart your success.

If you attend a group meeting weekly, report the results to your group.

WHY YOU GO THE EXTRA MILE

Although you take delight in outstanding service, in doing more than is expected and in making others feel good, be mindful most people operate the way they do because they personally benefit. There is nothing wrong with that, everyone feels the same. It would not make sense to render a service if there were not mutual benefits from doing the job.

The people who go the extra mile, beyond personal benefit, are the ones who have the slight edge to gain extra rewards. They are in demand, respected and appreciated in business and as individuals.

Think about it, in a race, the person who wins does it by a very slight edge. Seldom does anyone win by more than inches in a foot race. Watch the Olympics. The winners often win by seconds, by a nose. In other words, by just a little extra.

As you practice doing a little extra, you will be putting yourself in a position to be the leader in your field.

What is the little extra?

Know your sales presentation a little better than is required. Do it with a little more flourish. Be a little more considerate of others.

Know your product line a little better than required. Really know the results your product gets so you can give just a little more hope to your customers.

Know your marketing plan. Be able to recite it with feeling and enthusiasm. Express honest appreciation and genuine interest. You will build a stronger desire in others for what you are promoting. Increase, beyond average, the number of people with whom you talk.

What happens as you do these things? You feel good about yourself. You are the individual people look to and admire in your company. You are the leader in your field.

How does going the extra mile affect your personality? You feel good about yourself, you are in control, you are focusing on what counts, you are doing things right. You see the big picture and the pieces of the puzzle begin to fit. You are enjoying the rich, internal dimensions of life.

 **SUGGESTED ACTIVITY:**

Schedule five appointments. Before each appointment, study your presentation and product. See if you can make a little extra effort to offer a little extra information. Extend yourself in your presentation.

Tabulate your results and, if you attend a weekly group meeting, report the results to them.

UNDERSTANDING THE EXTRA MILE

There is little doubt that we all know the ways, whys and wherefores of the extra mile. That is just the beginning. The real value of the extra mile principle is the way we apply it to our own life. Apply this principle in your own way, to your own benefit, in every area of your life.

We have talked a lot about what going the extra mile means to others and how it affects their response to you, but how do you make this principle become a part of your personality and your philosophy? Matthew 5:41 says, "And whoever compels you to go one mile, go with him two." That is doubling up, that really gives you the edge and that is what is meant by "the extra mile." Do twice as much as expected. Wow! I wonder how many of us do that. I wonder what it would do to our business and to our personal life, if we did that!

How much do you expect of yourself? When you deliver the best service you feel you are capable of rendering, and then each time, strive to excel over what you have done in the past, you will draw out and develop from within you the forces of your mind and body which are available to you. Knowledge is power, only if used. We use a very small part of our wonderful brain because we do not ask for extra power.

Make it your chief aim to focus on surpassing all previous records you have set, beating all past performances, and you will develop a passion for surpassing yourself and for expecting the extra mile from yourself in all your endeavors. When you do this, life and work become a game and you are the player and the scorekeeper. You become so involved and so interested that you no longer feel you are doing the work, but you are playing the game. You take pride and joy in meeting the challenge, in beating the odds, in continually surprising yourself at just what you have in you. You love life and you live life to the fullest. **And, you are paid well for what you do because your love of the job and love of the challenge shows in the excellence of your performance, the countenance on your face and the positive expectancy of your personality. You become a well paid leader because you are doing more.** You have found the secret of living life to the fullest!

How do you want to be remembered? You have a legacy to leave. Make it the extra mile legacy and you will live on forever in the lives of others because of the example you have set. And you will have a wonderful time building that reputation!

℞ SUGGESTED ACTIVITY:

Pledge to yourself, from this day forward, to consistently go the extra mile for others and for yourself, to excel and to surpass each day the activity of the day before. Having pledged this, you will get more out of life, whether you actually excel day after day or not. You will have accomplished more for having made the commitment.

Personal Development

Personal Growth

AFFIRMATION:
I live each day in a calm, relaxed manner.
I am aware of my worth. I move forward confidently.
High energy is available to me through God,
who is working in my favor.

SELF-CONFIDENCE

Self-confidence is a trait we often see in others, but feel we do not have in ourselves. That is because we see deep inside ourselves and not into others. Approximately 98 percent of people who participated in a survey several years ago felt the personality trait they would most like to improve was self-confidence.

When you realize that you are not the only person who feels a lack of self-confidence, you are able to move ahead with a plan that will give you more security and more ability to develop your potential.

Knowledge gives you self-confidence. Have you ever noticed how hesitant you are on a new job or with a new idea or activity? Later, when you have really learned the procedure, you do the activity without hesitation. Spending too much time thinking about how you may or may not fail on a project will contribute to the lack of self-confidence. Fear sets in and you stop yourself before you get started.

It is important to your growth that you be **courageous**. This is not the absence of fear, but it is facing the unknown, learning the task and achieving your desired results by doing the thing you fear. Every time you do this, you are building your self-confidence, gaining knowledge and experiencing self-growth.

Get the action habit! A great hindrance to gaining confidence is doing nothing. Inactivity breeds fear, uncertainty and lack of confidence. It is very tiresome because, when you are doing nothing, you can't stop to rest!

SUGGESTED ACTIVITY:

Become more knowledgeable concerning your work. Start an intense study. As you study job skills, put them into practice, experimenting with the effectiveness of each new skill or procedure.

List a job activity that you would like to master, but are afraid you are not capable of doing. (This can be holding appointments to sell your product or opportunity, contacting people for appointments or any activity that makes you feel uncomfortable.) Forcing yourself to do this three times in a short time span will help you overcome your fear, build your confidence and develop a sense of excellence.

Do not despair, this will work for you. Daily affirm: "I can do this. Thank you, God, for helping me help others." This gets your mind off yourself as you think of others and you will gain courage. Your confidence will increase with each activity.

SELF-RELIANCE

Developing self-reliance may mean more to your personal growth than any other attribute you can achieve. Feeling confident that you can depend on yourself is a powerful feeling.

Concentrate on what you must do right now to build your *self-reliance*. Be mature, see the big picture. Accept the fact that you must work now to insure future rewards. Feel excitement for what your work holds and it becomes fun. Enthusiasm for what the future holds makes your work pleasurable. The more you work, the more you will enjoy your work and you will become self-confident, as you perfect your skills through experience.

In every activity that you consider, ask yourself, "Is this activity contributing to the development of my success and happiness?" Remember the words of Goethe: "He who has a firm will molds the world to himself."

When you take care of business, you will find your happiness level and your value to your loved ones increases. Consequently, your self-worth increases and you will feel a great sense of responsibility fulfilled. WHAT A LIFE YOU HAVE IN STORE! There is nothing to compare with the feeling, "I am accomplishing my mission in life."

℞ SUGGESTED ACTIVITY:

Make it a point to have at least one attempted success in your business activity every day.

Be persistent. If you quit, you will always wonder what would have happened had you continued.

Remember, the person who says, "It can't be done," is interrupted by the person who is doing it. Which one of these people do you want to be?

Have the determination to follow through with your resolve for success.

Get started! List all the rewards on the left side of a sheet of paper and the reasons not to get started on the right side of the same sheet. Which list is the largest?

Have a sense of urgency. Daily affirm: "Exceptional people produce their own urgent pressures. I am an exceptional person."

SELF-PERSEVERANCE

Perseverance equates to persistence. It is a very important trait in personal growth and achievement.

Everyone has down times, times when it seems nothing is going right and the only solution is "out." This is when people who have perseverance take heart. They know if they are feeling bumps in the road, they are going somewhere. They know if there are setbacks, there has to be advancements.

When you experience setbacks, it helps if you will remember to "give thanks for all things." Count your blessings. You will find you are doing very well! Tighten your belt and get the body in action. Any action will encourage persistence, whether it is holding appointments, making appointments or spending study time to learn how to do the job.

Where are you now? It takes perseverance to step on up, to be outstanding. Know you have the ability to do your best. Give it your all.

Think Up

Know, with perseverance, you can promote yourself to the very top.

Think Big

Expect more of yourself and your surroundings. Do not be hesitant to want more.

Communicate

Be sincere with yourself. Listen to yourself. Be sure your "self-talk" is positive.

Take it one step at a time. When you look at the whole picture and the total requirement, it is hard to persevere, but, little by little, you can accomplish the entire task and look back on your activity with pride of accomplishment.

Remove your limitations and judgments. Stay on track with the plan. Use the daily plan and activity sheet suggested earlier in this book.

℞ SUGGESTED ACTIVITY:

Review your goal plan. Are you on target? With your goal in mind, list your activities for last week. Itemize your accomplishments. Did you persevere or, if things did not go as planned, did you become discouraged and stop?

Make your weekly plan for this week, and add some activities. Be sure to break down activities into small increments. Perseverance is accomplished by taking one step at a time and tasting the victory.

Schedule three appointments that you consider "practice appointments," when you need encouragement. When you tell yourself you are practicing, you are less inclined to feel pressure. This will get you in the right frame of mind and convince you that you have the ability to continue forward and turn defeat into victory.

PERSONAL COMMITMENT

The commitment you make to yourself is most important. You are the only one who really knows what you want from life. If, at times you feel uncertain about the future, at least you know what you want today and tomorrow because you have a dream to fulfill.

To make that dream a reality, you must be willing to make personal commitments to do whatever it takes to achieve the dream. Remember, you are not going to get what you want, but you get what you expect! Make a commitment right now to receive the very best. Affirm to yourself: "I am committed to do what it takes to bring about my dream. With God's help, I know I will achieve success beyond my greatest expectations."

Having made your commitment, believe that you already possess the knowledge and the positive attitude to develop your skills. Every word you speak has power.

Self-commitment puts you in control of your life and your future. Once you are committed, you seem to create a magnet that attracts to you whatever you may need to reach your dream. You allow no one and nothing to keep you from achieving your heart's desire. You have made a pact with yourself and you respect yourself enough to keep that pact and follow through. This is self-commitment and it is more powerful than any commitment you can make to anyone.

Rx SUGGESTED ACTIVITY:

Write a letter to yourself. List all the achievements you are personally committed to accomplish within the year. Seal the letter and date the outside to be opened one year from now.

Write another letter to yourself. List all the achievements you are personally committed to accomplish within the next six months. Seal the letter and date the outside to be opened six months from now.

At the beginning of each month, for the next six months, write a letter to yourself listing, weekly, the activities necessary for you to perform to achieve your commitment.

Depending on the strength of your commitment, each week you will stretch to beat the week before, doing whatever is necessary to result in achieving your heart's desire. You will become known as an individual with a commitment to excellence and an example for all to follow. You will like it!

Positive Personality Traits

AFFIRMATION:
I look forward to the adventure of today as I develop and practice positive personality traits that are contributing to my success right now! By the grace of God, I have the ability, strength, desire and perseverance to bring out the best in myself.

IMAGINATION

The picturing power of the mind, soul and imagination creates self-confidence, initiative and leadership, and gives you a definite purpose in life.

Your success will come from:

THOUGHT IDEAS PLANS AND ACTIONS

Being keyed in to your imagination will give you that magic ingredient for the success which is born in the mind.

You have complete control of your imagination. No one can deprive you of whatever you choose to imagine. Good things imagined in life are manifested through your belief and action. The thoughts you put into your creative mind through imagination are transmitted to the conscious mind which directs the body toward that which you need to bring your imagined dreams into reality.

Positive imagination creates a magnet which attracts to you everything you need to fulfill your desire. People "pick up" on thoughts. Positive thoughts and positive images get back positive response, just as negative thoughts get negative response.

We constantly get ideas. Ideas and hunches acted upon can bring about tremendous results. Remember, every material thing you see was once an idea in someone's mind. Exciting, isn't it? Your marketing plan, the product you sell, the way you present it all stemmed from ideas and plans acted upon that were the product of someone's imagination.

SUGGESTED ACTIVITY:

What do you want to accomplish during the next three months? Crystallize your thinking, leave no room for doubt, write your definite purpose in no uncertain terms.

Imagine yourself completing the task. Visualize successful performance and positive results.

See yourself as you will be after you have accomplished this three-month achievement. For visual aid, prepare a chart with pictures representing **you** enjoying your success. Pictures of objects, awards or recognition you will be receiving will stimulate your imagination.

Pictures of people you will encounter and work with. Pictures of loved ones sharing your success will stir your emotions. In quiet moments, dwell on this imaging. Drift off to sleep at night with your imagination working for you. You will awaken in the morning aware of this image. Make this a lifetime habit and you will find the results of these thoughts will give you ideas and plans to promote yourself and your business. You will experience a very positive, pleasant outcome because you are putting forth the effort and performing the action stimulated by your imagination.

See yourself as the successful person you positively imagine you can become.

ENTHUSIASM

Henry Ford said, "You can do anything if you have enthusiasm. Enthusiasm is the yeast that makes your hopes rise to the stars. Enthusiasm is the spark in your eye, the swing in your gait, the grip of your hand, the irresistible surge of your will and your energy to execute your ideas. Enthusiasts are fighters, they have fortitude, they have staying qualities. Enthusiasm is at the bottom of all progress. With it, there is accomplishment. Without it, there are only alibis." Oh! To have those attributes describing you! Just think, with enthusiasm you can be the individual who exudes success to everyone you meet. Let's see what we can do to get this thing called enthusiasm.

Enthusiasm for your work is created through complete harmony with your belief in what you are doing. You have heard it said you cannot sell anyone anything in which you do not believe. The reason this is true is that you cannot sell anything without enthusiasm. If you are not sold on what you are selling, you cannot be enthusiastic with your presentation. Convince yourself that you represent the best company, product, opportunity and service available. Sell yourself on what you are doing, totally and unequivocally. Your belief creates the excitement that generates the enthusiasm. This is the first step to successful business.

Enthusiasm does not need to be displayed as loud and demonstrative, although that is certainly allowable and often practiced, and sometimes the physical activity generates enthusiasm. Enthusiasm quietly exudes in the way you carry yourself. Stand erect, shoulders back, tummy tucked in. Walk with definite purpose, self-assured in a controlled, quick pace. (Muggers hesitate to approach someone who is walking with a purpose. I think it is because they know that person is a winner and they will be a loser if they attempt anything with a person who has a purpose in life). Enthusiasm is projected by the look in your eye, the smile on your face, by your positive stance and by the set of your jaw! Enthusiasm is contagious so all the people with whom you come in contact will display enthusiasm. They will be excited about you, about the product you are selling, the opportunity you are sharing and they will want what you have. By projecting enthusiasm, you will become enthusiastic, and it will help you to persuade others, overcome your fears, make your job more rewarding, calm your nerves and help solve your problems. Enthusiasm is described as an intense feeling for a subject or cause. As you control your thoughts and your imagination, you will develop that intense feeling for life!

SUGGESTED ACTIVITY:

Check your enthusiasm level. If it is high, you want to keep it that way. If it is low, you must take steps to correct this attitude. It is within your power to do so. Daily, affirm "The energy is right for innovative ideas to come to my mind. I am prepared for a change for the better and I am entering into a state of higher awareness; I am open to inspiration and I am enthusiastic."

Physically pursue your career with eagerness. Get excited about it and enthusiastically carry on.

CONCENTRATION

Concentration means to fasten one's powers, effort and attention to obtaining the desire of one's heart or accomplishment of one's goal.

Concentration gives you the ability to focus your mind and effort on the task at hand, giving you the ways and means required to reach the results you desire.

The expression "cut to the chase" may apply here because concentration narrows it down to doing what is necessary and focusing on the job at hand.

Assuming you have made the decision to move ahead in your career, start practicing the habit of concentration. Keep your mind focused on the immediate task required to reach the next step of your career path. Crowd out all other thoughts that would detract from this action. "Put on the blinders" and keep moving straight ahead toward your accomplishment.

Stick to the job at hand. Do not allow yourself to become distracted by other tasks, do not listen to any negative suggestions and do not consider changing your plan until you have completed this step. You will then move on to the next step with confidence.

Set your path. Know what is required, have no doubt. Only then will you be able to give it your full concentration. Just reading the rules will not be enough to burn them in to your mind, you must write them and put them into practice.

Keep practicing your performance, both physically and mentally, until it becomes second nature. Then you will have formed the habit of concentration!

℞ SUGGESTED ACTIVITY:

Concentrate on showing your product, sharing your marketing plan. Practice this step physically at least five times as quickly together as possible. Practice this step mentally (imagine yourself doing it) at least twice a day.

You should be so focused on this that you do it with much less effort because you have formed the power of concentration. In the event you have not achieved this attitude, it will be necessary for you to concentrate on this step until you master the habit of doing it. Then, go on to the next step required on your career path, using the same procedure of concentration. The only drawback to perfecting your skill is the possibility that you may give a mechanical presentation. Be aware of this and practice the art of presentation with feeling, projecting your own personality, keeping the needs of others in mind.

This is really "learning your job by experience." By giving it your full concentration, you will know your job so well that success will come naturally and joyfully to you.

INTEREST

Who are you? Your personality traits, your appearance and characteristics are determined by your background, the thoughts you think, the clothes you wear, your attitude and actions. Your pleasing personality attracts and draws people to you. This is generated by subtle traits, not forced but very important.

SMILE. This is number one on the list because it is so easy and so important. People read you by your smile. Make it genuine. Really mean it when you smile. Let your smile crinkle your face and light up your eyes as it conveys the message "you are wonderful" to the other person. Some people think it is not professional to smile. They are wrong.

EYES. The eyes are the window of the soul. Eye contact is very important. Be aware of your thoughts and feelings because your mood and your intentions are reflected in the expression of the eyes. Often, people read you by your eyes. When you are excited and happy, the pupils enlarge. When you are afraid, angry or uncomfortable, the pupils are small.

VITALITY. It is important that your body movement be responsive, full of energy and gracious. This is reflected by the way you walk into a room, radiating energy. Vitality is expressed by the way you look at an individual, interested but not staring. Vitality is displayed by the way you shake hands, not too forceful, but firmly and caring, leaning toward that person.

TONE OF VOICE. Learn to speak directly, with conviction, yet softly and with inflection and reflection on your words. Speak from the heart, never use flattery, but be genuine in your compliments and show interest with your questions. To impress a person, talk about that individual's achievements, needs and desires, not your own.

BE AGREEABLE. Of course, you are entitled to your opinion, but you can be agreeable and bring other people around to your way of thinking much easier with gentleness than by argument or disagreement. See the situation from the other person's point of view and take it from there. Use the "feel, felt, found" system. "I know how you feel, I have felt the same way, but I have found, etc."

WEAR CLOTHES THAT COMPLIMENT your body style and that are suitable for the occasion. Proper grooming and dress contribute to the outside appearance and make a good first impression. If you don't get past first base because of your appearance, your pleasing personality may not have a chance.

All these traits reflect a heartfelt interest in other people. A genuine caring for them, their interests and needs and a real desire to serve them. People will say about you, "She/he really has a pleasing, attractive personality!"

SUGGESTED ACTIVITY:

Learn to express interest in other people. Contact five people and show genuine interest in them. Present your product or plan to them. Show them how it would be to their best interest to make a positive decision for what you have to offer.

Practice the ability to speak with force and conviction, vitality and gentleness. Recite your marketing plan into a tape recorder and play it back to yourself to monitor your tone of voice, inflection on words and genuine expression.

Stay positive. The only thing that can hold you back is the limitation you set in your mind. Release all limitations. Go forward and smile!

Notes

Persuasive Assertiveness

AFFIRMATION:
I communicate in an effective way for the benefit of all concerned, and I am able to use persuasive assertiveness in dealing with others. I think, believe and act in a way that is pleasing to others and, therefore, they will hear, accept and respect what I have to say.

DEVELOPING ASSERTIVENESS

People with high self-esteem are assertive in a persuasive way, which is a desirable trait. People with low self-esteem come across as aggressive, which is an undesirable trait. What message do you send? If you are not getting desired results in dealing with people, possibly, you are coming across as aggressive, even though your intentions are good.

How you feel, deep within, dictates your effectiveness in dealing with others, as well as your satisfaction with interactions. Self-worth, self-respect, self-confidence are essential to assertiveness. These are personality and attitude qualities of high self-esteem.

If you find people consistently resist you or that you seem to have a lot of conflict, possibly you are being aggressive and cannot accomplish the desired results, hurting your chances for success.

You may be experiencing a lack of self-worth, experiencing self-doubt and self-consciousness, causing you to be on the defensive and acting in an aggressive manner.

PRACTICE ACCEPTING YOURSELF AS YOU ARE. Concentrate on your personality assets and release your personality liabilities. Do not make excuses or defend yourself.

BUILD YOURSELF. Practice personal grooming and lifestyle appearance that validates you in your eyes, as well as in the eyes of others. Constantly be involved in a self-improvement, self-worth program through classes, books, tapes and positive experience. Do not hesitate to get counseling, if you feel you need it.

BE THE PERSON WHO IS "UP FRONT" IN THE GROUP. Stand and sit in prominent places to get the most out of the function you are attending. Participate with the group. Observe, listen and learn.

PRACTICE THE HABIT OF BEING ON TIME. Punctuality is an admirable trait and gives you credibility in the eyes of others. It keeps you from having last minute frustrations. Being on time will prevent embarrassment and dispel guilt feelings.

BE RESPONSIBLE. Follow through. Be as good as your word. This builds self-respect as well as respect others have for you and gives you confidence.

SHOW APPRECIATION. Make others feel appreciated and important. They, in turn, appreciate you and this builds self-esteem.

These activities build self-respect which is essential to self-esteem and will help you develop persuasive assertiveness.

Self-confidence, self-respect and self-esteem are essential personality traits for effective, assertive communication. Conversely, lack of self-confidence, self-respect and self-esteem cause aggressive communication and behavior.

 **SUGGESTED ACTIVITY:**

Review the above suggestions, write them on a lined pad. give yourself a score of 1 to 10, ten being the highest, to each suggestion. Total scores determine how you rate your actions.

Write a list of activities that you are going to improve or implement into your lifestyle that will help you develop your self-esteem and enable you to become more assertive.

Practice "being assertive." Ask a friend to rate and critique you on your approach. Take necessary steps to correct any unfavorable comments. Love your friend for being honest!

HOW TO BE ASSERTIVE

We are stimulated and effective when we are enthusiastically convinced that we are doing the right thing, selling the best product or offering the best opportunity.

To be persuasively assertive with others, we must first prepare and convince ourselves.

BE SURE OF YOURSELF. Know what you are doing. Do your research on the subject. Be sure your motives are in the best interest of all concerned. Be honest in your convictions.

KEEP YOUR LISTENER ON YOUR SIDE. Identify with your listener, and you will be able to interact pleasantly, causing your listener to be receptive.

TONE OF VOICE IS IMPORTANT. A firm, well-modulated voice signifies positive assertiveness. A shrill, loud voice can signify anger or it can signify fear and lack of self-confidence.

USE GOOD GRAMMAR. Expressions such as "Okay?" or "Agree?" at the end of a sentence can weaken your statement and project insecurity. Speak directly to the individual or group and use as few words as necessary to make the point.

BE POLITE BUT FIRM. Make eye contact, stand or sit straight. Keep a pleasant expression and control your voice. State your facts briefly and logically. Let your listener know that you stand by your convictions. Be willing to listen, but do not allow yourself to waiver.

GET YOUR LISTENER INVOLVED. Let your listeners know that you believe the idea you are presenting is to the benefit of all concerned. Get them involved by using nonthreatening prefaces to your ideas such as "How do you feel about...?" or "Don't you agree that...?" Keep in mind it is threatening to say "You should...." or "I want you to...." Rather, ask questions as suggested above or, if the case requires, say "I'm sure you agree, it would be to your best interest to...." Speak as if you expect others to take you seriously. Make your statement and stop talking.

People are persuaded into the action or decision you desire. They resist force. If you find yourself being too forceful, quickly get back on the persuasive track.

Effective assertion goes back to the same principle. Approach the subject from the other person's viewpoint and you will get your point across and your needs, wishes, desires will be met.

SUGGESTED ACTIVITY:

Make five sales presentations, keeping the rules you have just studied in mind. How do you feel about the results? Did you close more sales?

Applying the rules you have just studied, select someone you are very close to and attempt to "sell" that person on an idea you feel this individual basically opposes. Tread lightly. Be persuasively assertive.

WHY BE ASSERTIVE

ASSERTIVE PEOPLE ARE TREATED WITH RESPECT. Assertiveness comes as a result of self-respect. Self-respect demands the right to stand for your beliefs and to let other people know how you feel. When you use persuasive assertiveness, people will listen to you, as you make your feelings and convictions known. They will, in turn, take these thoughts into consideration with respect for you. When you are assertive and not aggressive, you are not on the defensive, so there is no argument in making your point. Your chances for making the point, making the sale or just stating the facts are positive and admirable, gaining respect. People never respect people they can "walk on."

ASSERTIVE PEOPLE HAVE THE ABILITY TO EXPRESS THEIR OWN OPINIONS. You have beliefs, opinions and rights. Express them in a firm, open way. So long as you are presenting your beliefs and not infringing on other people's beliefs, you will be persuasive. Stating your belief is much different than trying to make everyone think like you do, rather, you give others a right to have and express their opinions, just as you take that right. Good relationships are built in situations where each person knows and respects how the other feels.

ASSERTIVE PEOPLE HAVE THE ABILITY TO SET PRIORITIES. When you are assertive, you get control of your life. Set priorities and stick to them. Have the ability to say "no" and you gain respect and get things done. If you don't want to do something, or if you don't want to interrupt your schedule, say "no" and if the individual to whom you have said "no" tries to change your decision, stick to your guns. Remind yourself who is in charge of your life, actions and time.

 **SUGGESTED ACTIVITY:**

Think on past conflicts. How did you handle them? If you allowed someone else to take charge or if you declined in an aggressive manner, perhaps, there was anger involved at yourself or at the other person. Make a plan outlining how you will, with assertiveness, handle this situation in the future.

With practice, you can develop your skill of listening with empathy to help you know how your new behavior is affecting others. Be aware of how they are responding to you.

Stop trying to avoid conflict, anger and rejection by "giving in" to others. Accept responsibility for your feelings. Be honest with yourself and others.

Have five sales closings and five opportunity closings. Be aware of your assertiveness in these situations and keep a log of your results.

What keeps you from being assertive? Identify and correct. As you become comfortable with assertive skills, you will begin to use them efficiently in situations requiring quick responses. Continue to practice and be aware. In time, you will respond naturally, without thinking, and you will accomplish so much!

ASSERTIVE BODY LANGUAGE

We've all heard the defense used by the young man who committed indiscretions with the maiden: "Your lips said 'no, no,' but your eyes said, 'yes, yes'!" We also hear, "Your actions speak so loudly I can't hear what you say." There is good reason for this. It is estimated that 65 percent of our communication is nonverbal; only 35 percent verbal! Although most nonverbal communication is unconscious, a lot of it is understood! We need to become aware of the messages we silently convey.

Let's look at a few obvious communications through body language:

> Hands up, palms toward another individual signals pushing that person away from you. This is an aggressive, negative message.
>
> Shaking your finger at an individual is aggressive, antagonistic and threatening. It will cut off communication and arouse anger.
>
> Hands held up, fingers curled with palms toward you is a positive, assertive motion that says, "Come closer" or "Tell me more." It opens communication.
>
> A direct stance and direct eye contact with shoulders back,

arms at the sides signifies confidence, nonthreatening and persuasive, assertive body language.

Hugging oneself, shoulders pulled in and an indirect gaze signifies lack of confidence, fear, disinterest.

A good listening stance is leaning a little toward the individual who is talking, direct eye contact and mirroring the body language of the speaker (nodding the head with understanding, smiling and, in some instances, making notes). This stance is also good to use when you are convincing or selling.

Shrugging the shoulders shows lack of interest or inability to understand what is being said. This is usually considered a negative form of body language.

When sitting, if the legs are crossed with the top leg facing the individual sitting next to you, signifies a posture of acceptance. If it is facing opposite that individual, it signifies rejection.

Relaxed, uncrossed arms and legs signals acceptance. Crossed arms and legs signals rejection, lack of interest or fear.

These are just a few ideas. Make a study of body language. Watch people with whom you are dealing. See how their body language changes with interest or when you make them feel comfortable or uncomfortable. Be aware of your body language, especially when making a point.

SUGGESTED ACTIVITY:

It is important that your verbal language and your body language are compatible. Ask a friend to notice your body language and give you an opinion of what you say by your actions. Watch yourself in the mirror as you practice persuasive assertiveness. A video tape of yourself is a very effective way for you to study your body language.

Be aware of your body stance and body language. Stand straight, looking directly at people as you address them.

Focus on the issue. What is your goal? What do you want to accomplish? Make a list of how body language affects persuasive assertion. Will your body language help or hinder you in accomplishing your goal?

Notes

Getting It Fixed

AFFIRMATION:
By the grace of God, I have the power to grow, change what can be changed in my life and accept the things that cannot be changed. I do everything in my power to fix the character traits that are holding me back. I know I have as much "going for me" as anyone else, and I make a commitment to have a success attitude or "get it fixed."

STRESS

When we feel unable to meet our needs, socially or physically, we feel stress. If stress is allowed to overtake us because of continued inability to resolve conflicts, we become uncomfortable, insecure, and anxious, creating within us feelings of guilt and insecurity. This makes us disagreeable and unable to get along with people. Sometimes we retreat, withdrawing from others. Sometimes stress is relieved through anger.

People in business who are interested in success know they cannot express anger (it's not good for business!), nor can they afford to withdraw, allowing their feelings to stop them from pursuing their goals. Holding feelings within results in stress and that brings about many health and personality disorders.

Find a way to handle suppressed feelings such as anger, fear, hurt and many other sensitivities. Here are some ideas:

IDENTIFY YOUR PROBLEM. Ask yourself questions. Often stress is caused by worrying about something that may never happen. It is estimated that 97 percent of what we worry about never comes to pass. Write down what is bothering you. Just putting it on paper tends to minimize it. Now, think about the worst thing that can happen if this actually comes to pass. Condition yourself to accept it, but immediately go to work on ways to improve the situation.

ORGANIZE YOUR LIFE AS MUCH AS POSSIBLE. Plan your days and follow a simple routine as efficiently as possible. Delegate anything someone else can handle to relieve your workload. Clear your schedule and you clear your mind, alleviating a lot of stress.

LEARN TO MAKE DECISIONS. Indecision leads to procrastination and frustration. Making no decision puts you in "limbo" and, in most cases, it can be worse than making the wrong decision. Once a decision is made, have a plan, follow the plan with a sense of controlled urgency.

KEEP ACTIVE. When you feel stress, temporarily stop what you are doing. Use your power to change routines, habits and reach for new experiences, new people, new activities. In severe stress, excess physical activity such as punching bags, exercise, cleaning house, etc., often works it out, relaxes the body and clears the mind, putting you in condition to reevaluate and handle the cause of stress.

℞ SUGGESTED ACTIVITY:

If you do have a stress attack:

SPEAK UP. Do not hesitate to make your ideas and suggestions known. Feel worthy, stand up and be counted.

BE RESPONSIBLE. Face the facts. Do what is right. If you make a mistake, admit it, correct it and don't do it again.

BE SELF-RELIANT. Stay away from mind-altering drugs. They mask the problem and make it worse.

Face the situation. Don't retreat. Have faith. You can handle it. Be courageous, you have strength. Daydream good outcomes. Review your goals. Associate with people. Take a break! Play! Smile! Laugh! Laughter, even forced laughter, releases tension and helps stress. Work. Sometimes work is the best medicine.

FEAR

Each individual seems to have different fears. Basically, a small amount of fear is good and can become stimulating to move a person in the right direction. Unfortunately, if not dealt with, most fears gradually take over and kill enthusiasm, destroying initiative, purpose and ambition.

I have noticed when individuals need to be at their best because of crisis, disappointment or lack of initiative, they seem to become immobilized, unable to perform their duties. This is because they fear loss of social or economic status due to the situation that provoked the fear and caused their loss of self-respect.

Signs of extreme fear are exhibited by discontent, uncertainty and indecision. Fears are very important and very real. They can become a driving force. If allowed to take over, they will rob you of success and happiness. Fear can immobilize you and make it impossible for you to do the work and follow your plan. Fear can affect your mental state, rob you of personal happiness, affect your personality and make you physically ill. There is no end to the damage fear can accomplish. It is imperative that you deal with this culprit by recognizing your fears and handling them.

Identify your fears. Admit them. Make a written list of each fear. Spend a few minutes to get them completely in your mind. Separate these fears into the following categories:

FEAR OF THINGS BEYOND YOUR CONTROL. Write a list and release the fear. Faith is the opposite of fear. Admit you can do nothing about this situation. It is beyond your control and ask God to handle it for you. Thank God for the things you can control with His help.

FEAR OF THINGS THAT ARE WITHIN YOUR CONTROL. Write a list and identify your fear. Write beside each fear why you feel the way you do. Once you have identified your fear and determine why you have it, you can make a plan of action to overcome the fear. You will find most of these fears are mental and not physical.

DEVELOP A POSITIVE MENTAL ATTITUDE CONCERNING FEAR. Often, mentally, physically and emotionally we are so concerned that we make fear affirmations, bringing on ourselves the thing we fear the most. When you find yourself dwelling on the fear and worry of what might happen, quickly turn your thoughts around and concentrate on the positive side of the fear. Memorize positive affirmations so that you can call them into your mind the minute fear thoughts creep in. Know the mind can handle only one thought at a time. Make this a faith thought and not a fear thought.

DO THE THING YOU FEAR MOST AND THE FEAR WILL PASS. I know this is a cliché, but it is very true! When you set up a plan of action to do the thing you fear, you will agree that this is the best way to overcome fear. This activity equates to growth. Start with your smaller fears and purposely put yourself in a position to overcome them by attacking them with gusto. As you overcome the small fears, you will gain confidence to take on greater challenges. You will feel good and become more effective, as you gain control over your life by gaining control over fear.

FOLLOW YOUR DREAM. Break the fear habit and you overcome limited thinking. Dream big and don't be afraid to pursue the dream. Act as if nothing can keep you from having your heart's desire. Do what is necessary, widen your horizons, create new desires, embark on training courses to expand your ability. You are never too old to learn and to change. Be daring, step out in faith and claim what is yours. Continually tell yourself "I can do it!"

 **SUGGESTED ACTIVITY:**

Make your fear list. From this list, take one fear at a time. Work on overcoming that specific fear. Reach out to five people who have been intimidating to you. Pursue an activity you have been afraid to do in the past. Start slowly and you will grow bolder as you progress.

SELF-IMAGE

How do you see yourself? Are you so "wrapped up" in yourself that you often forget others? Self-conscious people have a low self-image. It is a little like wearing clothes that don't fit. All we can think about is how uncomfortable we are. We fret about how we look and feel. We are so busy thinking about this that we cannot concentrate on self-respect or the needs of others.

How you understand yourself dictates the way you react to people around you. It is important to direct your emotions into productive channels and develop personality patterns which make you acceptable to others.

LIGHTEN UP. Stop taking yourself so seriously. Turn your fears, worries and frustrations into positive energy through emotion control.

LOOK INTO YOURSELF. Search your mind. What do you think of yourself? This can often be defined by what you think of others. What do you fear about others? This may be defined as what you fear about your inabilities.

If you can embrace this one thought: *"See the good in others as you would like them to see the good in you,"* you will have solved the majority of your self-image problems. I believe it is true that the world gives back to us what we give out to the world.

Never criticize, always praise. Never curse, always bless. Reach out to others with a smile—it is a universal language and is always acceptable.

Don't concentrate on defeat, but acknowledge, that when you make progress, some defeat is inevitable and you can win over defeat by utilizing your energy. Concentrating and acting on achieving your goals will restore your self-image and you will overcome attitudes of defeat and continue onward to success.

No one has 100 percent success with their plan for life. Instead of allowing small defeats to give you a sense of inferiority, guilt and fear, take them in your stride, learn from them, use them as stepping stones. Success most often is just beyond small defeats and, in retrospect, you will be able to see what an important part the small setbacks played in your growth and success. Give thanks, pull on your faith and carry on to victory. This gives your self-image a tremendous boost.

Learn to manage your emotions. Anger, fear, pettiness, self-pity and any negative emotion that drains vitality makes you hostile, chronically tired, tense and unable to get along with others.

℞ SUGGESTED ACTIVITY:

Concentrate on your strengths, not your weaknesses. Using two columns, in one column make a list of your strengths; in the other column make a list of areas in which you feel weakness. Do not magnetize the weakness by giving it priority, but make a plan to do what it takes to overcome the weakness.

Concentrate on your victories, not your losses. Make a list of your victories. Acknowledge your losses and investigate why you had them. Do not dwell on them or grieve over them, but learn from them.

Concentrate on your powers, not your problems.

Take action. Make five business appointments and follow through with activity to build your success and your self-image.

FAITH

Faith is belief. Faith gives hope for things to come. It is putting aside logic and trusting in that which is unseen.

PLACE YOUR FAITH IN THINGS THAT COUNT

BELIEVE IN GOD. This gives you super natural power, and is the basis for all faith. When you embrace this faith in power unseen, but believed, you have a limitless supply which never fails. Practicing celestial faith enables you to practice temporal faith.

BELIEVE IN YOURSELF. You have abilities beyond all you can imagine. Never allow doubt to bring you down. Know you are created for a purpose and you have the power, through faith, to achieve the desires of your heart. Faith gives you confidence to reach out, to look up, to stand tall and to have it all.

BELIEVE IN YOUR COMPANY. Be informed, know the mission of your company and take responsibility to do your part to uphold the mission. Through faith, be involved with your company's progress and work as though the success of the entire company depends on you. This gives you pride and loyalty and insures your personal success. It also helps you instill faith in others.

BELIEVE IN YOUR PRODUCT AND SERVICE. Know you have the best. Cherish it and love it. Through faith, you will project enthusiasm and enjoyment for all you do and this will attract clientele, business associates, happiness and success.

HOW TO DEVELOP FAITH

It is impossible to develop faith using logic. One must throw caution to the winds and allow themselves to trust their instincts, to believe the unbelievable. Faith is spiritual. It cannot be forced, but it will flow freely when you let go and let God.

BE INFORMED.

- Read the Holy Bible for faith in God. Learn trust through prayer.
- Read your business guide for faith in your company. Really know your company philosophy. Know your job and what is required of you.
- Study your product and service. Know what makes it work. Practice with it, become really sold on it. The more you do, the greater the faith. As you see results, your faith is strengthened. Strong faith gives you credibility and makes you believable, and people will want what you have to offer.

SUGGESTED ACTIVITY:

To increase your faith spiritually, read the Holy Bible. Hebrews, Chapter 11 gives awesome examples of faith.

To increase faith in yourself, review your past positive performances and outcomes. Dream about your potential and make the dreams reality by doing the work that is required.

Remember to project the enthusiasm and positive attitude that faith brings, as you make the presentation. Your faith in your product and/or service is evident by your actions, words and body language.

Review your work and make a commitment to consistently have faith and to do what is required to realize your impossible dream.

Putting It Together

AFFIRMATION:
I know I never stop growing and learning.
I hereby commit myself to be open to learning,
to accept criticism, to appreciate compliments and to
become physically and emotionally strong enough
to make a difference in my life and in the lives of others.

FORMULATE

ABRAHAM LINCOLN SAID:
"DETERMINE THAT THE THING CAN AND SHALL BE DONE, AND THEN WE SHALL FIND THE WAY."

Before you can **formulate**, it is necessary to **believe** that what you want to happen can come to pass because you are willing to pay the price to make it happen. Then, things will open up to you.

Do not limit your plans to wishes and remain in the dream stage, but have purpose to set your plan in motion.

ASK YOURSELF, "Who is in charge of my life?" God gave you the ability to make choices. The choices you make determine what happens in your life. When you develop a chameleon personality, changing your ways and plans depending on who you are with, or living to please others, you become over adaptive and vulnerable to peer pressure. This results in confusion and ineffectiveness in your life.

FORMULATE A DEFINITE PLAN. Review your goal plan and your plan of action. Using your daily plan of action gets you off to a good start each day allowing you to get more accomplished as you attend to your business consistently. Consequently, you will have more time for self-improvement and enjoyment each day. You are less likely to be swayed to waste time or to be sidetracked from your main purpose for the day.

ACCEPT YOURSELF. You may respect other people's ideas and their opinions of you, but you need not be dependent on them. When you accept yourself, you are able to pull on your strengths and improve your weaknesses. Recognizing your worth gives you the ability to make the right decisions and the right connections, empowering you to stand by your convictions.

COOPERATE WITH OTHERS, but do not allow others to run your life. It is important that you develop into the type of person who works effectively with others as well as expecting them to work with you.

SUGGESTED ACTIVITY:

Review this message.

Check your plan for the day. Are you making a written plan? Do so for the next 21 days. After 21 days you will have formed a positive habit.

Write a list of things you like about yourself. Write a list of things you dislike about yourself. Make lists of your strong points and weak points. Make a plan of action to develop strengths from weak points.

CONCENTRATE

Pay close attention to your motives and to what is going on around you. How do you influence the world? What is the mark you will leave? What impact will you have on the lives of others? When you focus on these ideas, you are sure to have a more meaningful, more productive, happier life.

Learn to regulate and discipline yourself through the exercise of alertness and reason.

When you have a rational ground or motive for your actions, you will forge ahead, overcoming fear, inertia and indifference.

You will have the fortitude to endure physical or mental hardships or sufferings without giving up and feeling defeat.

You will have firmness of mind and will be able to meet danger or adversity.

You will have courage and staying power. That is what it takes to get the job done and to experience triumph.

As you get caught up in your plan, use moderation. You can accomplish your dreams and keep your balance, as well as protect your integrity. Be just and fair in your dealings with others, conform to the rules of justice. Do the right thing.

Trust in God is mighty and it will give you hope and strength to believe your desire is obtainable. It is inconceivable that anything good can be accomplished without trust in God. This makes all things possible.

Faith and trust also leads to love. Practice tolerance of others and stress goodwill in serving others, while fulfilling your plan. Balance your motives for the good of all concerned.

Concentrate your physical efforts in a definite plan of continuous action. It is not possible to accomplish what you want by starts and stops. It is consistency that wins in the end.

 **SUGGESTED ACTIVITY:**

Review your plan. Emphasize consistency.

Continually renew your faith through study and practice.

Schedule appointments that will require concentration on service and filling the needs of others.

After each appointment, review your performance, what you are accomplishing and how you feel about your progress. Ideally, you will feel a sense of growth and satisfaction for yourself, as well as for those you served.

INSTIGATE

As you impel yourself forward into action, your imagination will be stirred. All great ideas, all great success, starts in the mind.

So often we live in limitations due to the lack of belief, faith, will and ambition.

Instigation brings about a catalyst of incentive and stimulation and leads to personal initiative upon which you build your future.

Personal incentive will keep you abreast and ahead of what is happening. You will be open to new ideas, new opportunities and you will enhance the system and standards which have already been set.

In this world, there are people who are not content to stay in a rut. They may seem eccentric or risk takers to others, but they are the people who forge ahead and come up with new ideas, new ways and means of accomplishment, and they are leaders in their field.

I have heard it said, "If you have a plan that has been tested and is working, follow along. Don't reinvent the wheel. Don't rock the boat." I agree, up to a point. Embrace the plan that you know works, but see if there is a way that you can improve, not necessarily change, that plan. Can you tailor your presentation to be a little more awe inspiring, a little more dramatic? Can you go the extra mile and do a little more than is expected? Can you stand out from the crowd?

Be an instigator for good, for improvement, by searching for better ways, and you will be rewarded with the feeling that you have reason for living. You will discover dedication to and for your mission in life.

As an instigator, you are self-motivated. You are so excited about excelling beyond ordinary standards and stretching your capabilities that you have the initiative to go after what you see, make a plan, take the risk and be the winner in your field.

℞ SUGGESTED ACTIVITY:

Study your work habits. Are you just meeting standard requirements of your job? Are you just getting by? See what you can do to get yourself more excited, exciting and excitable. Organize your activities accordingly.

How is your presentation? Do you present your product with enthusiasm? Do you really care about the people to whom you are making your presentation? Is your presentation a little more dramatic than average? How can you improve? Double up on your sales calls and your marketing talks. Put a little more personality into your presentation.

Study your marketing plan and your product. Do you know all there is to know about the company and product you represent? Do you have good ideas for the enhancement of the plan or product? Don't be afraid to make suggestions to your company for positive changes. Many companies use and enhance their plan, accepting ideas such as yours.

PARTICIPATE

It is easy to take part, to share, to be associated with others. The important thing to consider is whether or not the participation is promoting what you want to achieve for yourself and others.

HAVE A DEFINITE LIST OF ACTIVITY PRIORITIES:

There are so many activities available today, it is very easy to become involved. It is important to set priorities on activities in which you participate and be sure they are in harmony with your plan for life and your plan for business. When in doubt or when tempted to engage in an activity that is questionable, ask yourself: "Is this activity contributing to my desire for success? Is this activity consistent to my station in life? Will this activity set a good example for others?" If the answer is "no," then have the courage to graciously say "no" to the desire for the activity.

Participate in activities of successful people, run with the winners! Spend no time in worthless activity. Participate and attend meetings, workshops, seminars and training activities. Participation with others who are in the same business and of the same faith as you, will add to your experience and is surely worthwhile. Take joy in participation.

Share your knowledge and your time in worthwhile activities. Do not be concerned about who gets the credit for the deed or the idea, as long as the job gets done. Your rewards will come.

Group participation with optimists can be your most motivating factor and it certainly is an education to associate with people who have similar goal plans as you. Be a part of the group, contribute, be dependable and participate!

SUGGESTED ACTIVITY:

Review your business goals. Make certain you are definite and precise on what you want, and how much time you need to devote to achieve your desire.

Check with your peers, your leaders and associates to see if there are any activities in which you need to be participating.

Put a sign by your phone which reads: "Will this activity contribute to the achievement of my goals?"

Get involved with your business. Schedule extra appointments, more than you feel you can handle, and participate with enthusiasm to accomplish more than ever before.

Latch on to your ideas. Write them down as they come to you, otherwise, they may be lost or forgotten. Keep a pencil and pad or a tape recorder at your bedside so you can record these great ideas that awaken you at 3:00 AM.

℞

The Balancing Act

AFFIRMATION:
I am centered, calm and balanced, even in the midst of chaos, because I know what I want. My energies and desires are a perfect blend. I know the importance of keeping my priorities under control and I am always aware of keeping harmony in my life, at home and on the job.

WHAT'S THE POINT

Do you sometimes feel like a juggler? Running and jumping to keep all the balls in the air and, at the same time, wondering which one you can eliminate?

Are you wearing more hats than you can handle? Do you sometimes forget which hat you have on and why?

While it is great to be thankful for the bounty of work and home, there are times when one has to stop and ponder: Why do you work? Most people are so busy working, they forget why. Consider these reasons:

A MATTER OF NECESSITY. We work to pay our way in life. To eat. To provide shelter for ourselves and our loved ones.

A MATTER OF CHOICE. We work for the joy of it. For escape. For personal growth. For rewards and recognition.

A MATTER OF LIFE ENHANCEMENT. We work to better ourselves and our family. If our needs are supplied by another means, our work affords the extras.

These are a few specific reasons people work. There are widespread motives, but more than likely these are the "big three."

To enjoy balance, success and happiness, it is wonderful if you can combine these reasons to work.

Regardless of how necessary it is to work or how mundane your work may be, combine the necessity to provide the needs by exercising the choice to enjoy what you do.

Take personal pride in the job you are doing. Even if your job has no incentives, give yourself incentive to feel the satisfaction of doing your best. If you get no rewards from your company, reward yourself. Give yourself a sales goal, target date or any incentive to reward yourself for doing a great job.

Look for ways you can grow and improve and keep a positive outlook for betterment. You will then be enjoying life enhancement.

Some of the richest people I know are on the low end of the pay scale. They are rich in spirit, they do their best and somehow their needs are always met. Happiness seems to be their trademark.

SUGGESTED ACTIVITY:

Examine the reasons why you work. Write a short essay to yourself listing and elaborating on these reasons.

List activities and rewards you like about your work.

List job requirements and activities you don't like about your work.

Find ways to eliminate or accept these dislikes.

List job requirements and activities about your work that make you uncomfortable, intimidated or afraid. Make a conscious effort to perform these activities and meet the job requirements.

Purposely prepare these lists and do these activities to help you overcome the feelings you have. Actively working your list will help you overcome your feelings of discomfort, uncertainty and fear.

ENJOYING HOME

"HOME IS WHERE THE HEART IS"—"EVERY MAN'S HOME IS HIS CASTLE"—"THERE'S NO PLACE LIKE HOME" are just a few of the sentiments we have heard through the years.

Perhaps the dream in life is to have a comfortable, secure place to call home. A home that protects us from intrusion and shelters us from the outside world. Home is a place that allows us to relax, create and be ourselves without fear of criticism.

Perhaps most of the money we earn from working is spent toward the cost, upkeep and furnishings of our homes. To have and to live in a pleasant home is a very motivating factor to work.

Complete separation of work from home is not always possible or advisable. Your identity and activity is basically the same, 24 hours a day, but to make yourself interesting and interested, to be more productive and to enjoy work and home, some division must be made.

If you happen to be in direct sales, self-employed or have your office in your home, planning is essential.

Establish definite working hours, scheduling them at the peak of your personal body productive time. If your work involves dealing with the public, your working hours need to be at appropriate times to reach other individuals during their working hours.

Determine and plan your working hours on a written format. It is usually best to project this weekly, listing daily activities, hours and demands as suggested in the chapter on "Time Management Made Easy" in this book. This helps you to live in day-tight compartments and frees you to feel comfortable about the hours you have planned for personal "home" time. It gives you the freedom to "work when your work" and "play when you play."

Always remember, it is necessary, daily, to take some quality time for yourself. Planning personal freedom time allows for enjoyment with a clear conscious, makes you happier, more enjoyable and more productive when you are working or enjoying family time.

I have often been amazed as I have observed people in some countries in Europe. They seem to get so much accomplished and have a great time doing it. They start their day early, work until noon and then take two to three hours off midday to relax, rest and enjoy. They go back to work from 3:00 PM until 9:00 PM, then they are off for the late evening. They seem to get a lot done this way and have time for themselves. They seem to get two days out of one. Surely, this takes planning on their part.

SUGGESTED ACTIVITY:

Organize your work on a consistent weekly basis. Prepare seven squares. Divide each square into four equal parts. Classify the parts as spiritual, personal, family, business. Each day, tabulate the percentage of time you devoted to each of these categories. Are you pleased with the balance? If not, do what you can to reorganize.

BALANCING STRESSFUL SITUATIONS

Every time you make a decision, ask yourself, "How does this fit into my lifestyle? How does it contribute to meeting my goal? How important is this activity to me and my enjoyment? How necessary is it to my success?" A lot of energy is spent doing things you feel you "should" do because someone else expects it of you. Possibly this is the main cause of stress in your life.

Stress is often caused by committing yourself to activities beyond your ability or time limits because you are unable to say "no" to others or to yourself. Proper planning will eliminate this hazard because you are taking control of your life.

Learn to prioritize your responsibilities. Divide situations in two categories: Situations you can control, and situations you can't control. When you feel stress, analyze and see from which category your stress originates. If it is brought about by something you can control or change, then by all means, change immediately or suffer the consequences. You will be surprised how much you can change as you become aware of this choice you have made to be in control of your life. If your stress is brought about by something you cannot change, accept the situation or condition and learn to cope with it. Acceptance is a big step toward coping. Continually trying to control something over which you have no power causes more stress. In situations such as this, let go and let God. Release does wonders and you will be amazed at the effect it has on you and your ability to cope. Many stressful situations resolve themselves when you practice this exercise.

There are areas in your life which you can control. For example: if your workload is too heavy, control this by finding someone you can pay to do some of the work. You do not have to do it all. It really does not matter who does the task, so long as it is accomplished. Hiring good help is the best investment you can make, both in the home and in the office. This relieves stress and frees you to utilize your talent for greater accomplishments and enjoyment.

Attempting to change a situation or an individual over which you have no control, brings extreme stress. Let go. Acknowledge that you are not God and this is His department. You will have freedom to grow in areas that are yours to control and handle.

Planning is a major key to leading a balanced life. When you plan ahead, you are in control and you will be able to handle disruptions and interruptions.

SUGGESTED ACTIVITY:

List stressful situations which cause imbalance in your life.

Examine each one carefully to see if you can correct it or if it is something you need to release.

Ask yourself about each situation: Will it matter a week from now? A year from now? Five years from now? You will find, having answered these questions, most situations are not as important as you make them.

BALANCING YOUR LIFE

Often our lives are out of balance simply because we have failed to evaluate the four major areas that are necessary for balance. Let's look at them, one at a time.

SPIRITUAL LIFE. Matthew Chapter 6, Verse 33, "Seek ye first the Kingdom of God and His righteousness and all these things shall be added unto you," leaves no doubt about the first priority in your life. First and foremost, respect and practice your belief in God, putting him first in your life, read his word, pray and have fellowship with fellow believers on a regular basis. Putting this area of your life first gives you unlimited strength and peace that passes understanding.

SELF. Yes, that is right, self must have high priority. So often self is overlooked. You must provide for yourself before you can provide for others. You must love yourself in order to love others. That does not mean that you are puffed up or in love with yourself, but that you have a healthy self-respect and self-responsibility. Do what is necessary to have a healthy body and mind. Be the master of your body with proper diet and exercise and forsake habits that can destroy you. Avoid stress by keeping your priorities straight.

FAMILY. Everyone needs someone to provide for, someone to love. If you have no family, then develop an extended family of friends or causes that you can support. If you are a spouse and a parent, consider your family before all others and let them know they can depend on you. Include your family in your plans and let them know your goals and desires for yourself and for them. Set aside quality time for these people who mean the most to you.

CAREER. Having a reason to get up in the morning, having motivation to excel really adds fuel to your fire and keeps you going. Love what you are doing and continue to find ways to excel over what you have accomplished in the past. If you have no paying career, then find an avocation, a hobby or a cause in which you can become interested. Everyone needs the feeling of accomplishment.

These are the four ares in your life that must be balanced in order for you to enjoy work, home and life in general. As you think of these four areas, it is impossible to separate them in your life, so consider them on a horizontal line, not a vertical line. Consider that they all have equal time because you are living each one of these areas 24 hours a day, seven days a week, and it takes all four areas to make you complete. Some days you will spend more time on one area than on the other, but, usually, when you are spending time in one area, it enhances the other area of your life because it affects your total person.

An example of this can be: ***Career Time***. Doing your job actually enhances ***you*** because you have a personal sense of satisfaction from your work and pay for service rendered. It enhances your ***family*** because it is a means of your financial support and devotion to them and, by your actions, your ***spiritual life*** can be glorified as a testimony for what you believe. Consequently, these areas are like the four fingers on the glove and the thumb is the balancing measure, keeping your life in order.

℞ SUGGESTED ACTIVITY:

Look at the four areas in your life. List how they affect each other. Check to see if you are setting your priorities straight in all four areas. Do whatever is necessary to balance these areas.

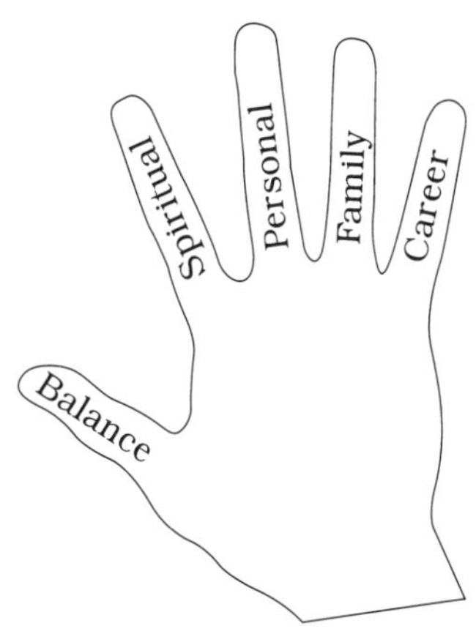

Notes

℞

Attitude Development

Dealing with Apathy

AFFIRMATION:
I have so much to achieve and I am enjoying every step of the way. I have great expectations, a map, a guide and a healthy attitude for my life's work. Each day is a new, exciting experience, thanks to God!

BOREDOM

Feeling the lack of emotional responsiveness or apathy is no respecter of persons. It can happen to any of us.

Boredom is possibly the main cause of apathy. Have you ever seen anyone who is moving ahead, achieving goals, gaining recognition and earning money show signs of apathy? I haven't. Real achievers are not bored because they have:

1. **Faith in God that sustains and encourages, in good times and bad.**
2. **A map or guide for achievement.**
3. **Self-discipline which gives the ability to direct the mind which, in turn, directs the body into action.**

4. **Excitement to face problems, knowing every problem shows progress and is an opportunity for growth. Facing problems always generates strength.**
5. **Tolerance. Have common sense. Have no tolerance for wife beaters, child abusers, subversive organizations or movements, etc.**

These five steps will give you continued education and the ability to attain the desired purpose with freedom and enjoyment.

Get excited about other people's good fortune. Positive, happy feelings about the success of others is invigorating and builds your personality. Resentment is dangerous and will adversely affect your behavior.

SUGGESTED ACTIVITY:

Make a list of people who have been instrumental in your continual education. Write a note of appreciation to each of them.

Make three contacts each day which will give you experience in your life's work.

Make a "dream list" of achievements that you can get excited about.

Be open and excited about all individuals and activities in your line of work.

Be happy, relax, laugh! Enjoy!

APPRECIATION

Count your blessings! Concentrate on what you have, not on what you lack.

Remember the story about the people who brought their cares, concerns and worries to the town square to exchange with each other. Each individual was excited about taking home a lighter bag of trouble. When the display was examined, they each were thankful to pick up the bag they had brought.

Is your job boring? Not giving you satisfaction? Holding you back? Look around—seek something better. Chances are you have the best, but if you don't feel that way, don't be afraid to change. Do not change until you feel you have done your best and made necessary personality changes. Some people are not happy anywhere. It's not the environment, but trouble within the individual. That person can continually change jobs (and often does) and never be happy. Take responsibility for your own happiness and you'll find life treats you better.

If you are in direct sales, check the marketing plan and product. See if there are ways to make new approaches. Are you giving it your all? Are you motivated to enhance your position? Do not just find fault, find solutions.

Sometimes just a little appreciation, counting your blessings is all you need to turn yourself around and make the most of what you have.

It is possible to be disappointed with the people in your life. They may not show you the consideration and/or respect you deserve. It never seems to help when you criticize people for this lack or when you remind them of their faults. Instead, find an admirable quality, even if they slightly possess it, or a quality you want them to develop. Compliment and praise them for this quality and watch them change! People usually live up to your expectations. It is like magic!

 **SUGGESTED ACTIVITY:**

Consciously show appreciation for your work, product and to the people with whom and for whom you work. When you show appreciation, you get appreciation.

Work. It is the best therapy. Activity cures anxiety and apathy, and makes life exciting and profitable. You will recharge your battery and put wind in your sails!

Take heart. Things are never so bad they can't get worse; never so good they can't get better, and this too shall pass.

PLANNING

Planning promotes harmony in your life and in the lives of others. Take time to plan. When you have made a long-term plan for your life, apathy is less likely because you continue to look ahead and press forward.

Planning promotes harmony with others because you have scheduled time for spiritual, personal, family and work activity.

Planning gives balance to life. A weekly plan takes off pressure and a daily plan helps you live in day-tight compartments. All accomplishment is planned ahead but achieved one day at a time. Living from day-to-day toward a goal lowers the likelihood of apathy because you always look forward to tomorrow.

Planning prevents frustration. Feeling you have more to do than you can accomplish promotes apathy because you feel you are doing the impossible. On the other hand, it seems **always** possible to handle the activity for one task at a time, one day at a time. You can make it through *this* day.

Planning helps dispel fear. It is not so frightening or overwhelming to contemplate what you must do to achieve your goal, if you have written it in "bite size" activities.

Planning gives hope. Hope is faith for things not seen. Planning gives you something to look forward to with faith and anticipation.

SUGGESTED ACTIVITY:

Review your long-term and short-term activity goals.

Review your daily plan sheet. Be sure you have divided activities into categories that must be done, should be done and activities that can wait. Daily, tackle activities in that order.

Prepare a personal plan sheet for the week ahead, listing what you will wear each day and for each activity. See that the clothes you plan to wear are clean and in repair, and at the end of each day lay out what you will wear the next day. You will be amazed at the time you save and how well-groomed you are when you use this method. When you are traveling, follow the same plan as above to have your clothes well-organized for packing and for wearing while on a trip. This would also apply to toilet articles, makeup, etc. Keep clutter out of your life as much as possible. Planning ahead makes this happen.

PROJECTS

Having a project to complete gives energy to keep moving and inspiration to look ahead. Continuous projects concerning your faith, family and career as well as self-improvement are essential to your well-being.

Strengthen your faith. A strong faith releases your creative power. Faith, linked with prayer, opens endless reservoirs of knowledge and gives you unlimited vitality for life. Faith is strengthened through prayer, through reading the Holy Bible and through associating with others of strong faith. Faith is strengthened by knowledge and knowledge comes through study. Daily reading of inspirational material and daily meditation on spiritual and physical goals gives strength.

Share your good fortune and faith with others. Rewards come when you least expect them. The humble spirit reaps gain.

Get your family involved with your work. Share your goals, your commitment and your need for their support. Help them to feel connected and accountable. Delegate tasks that will make them feel included in your work. Share with them your good fortune and project a positive outlook. Keep your troubles to yourself, if at all possible. You can work through the hard times, but your family feels at a loss to know how to help you and can make the trouble seem worse than it is. Or, they can give you too much sympathy and encourage your defeated feelings.

Always have a self-improvement program that is projected to help you grow as an individual and as a career person.

Talk with people who have achieved what you want to accomplish in your career. Learn from their mistakes and victories. Attend meetings, seminars and classes concerning your line of work. Read biographies of successful people.

Be aware of your health and have a plan that will give you vitality, keep you healthy and good looking. It is hard to have a good attitude, be enthusiastic and feel like working when you are not feeling well or if your body is in a "slump." Take a good look at yourself. Are your eating habits good? Are you taking vitamin supplements? Do you have an annual check up? These are things you owe yourself and those you love if you are to live a happy, successful life.

When you have a project that promotes growth in all areas of your life, you are most unlikely to ever suffer apathy. Life is too exciting and you look forward to it each new day.

SUGGESTED ACTIVITY:

Review the suggestions made in this program.

List all suggested activities mentioned and carry them out, tailoring them to your need and position at this time.

Special Note: When you read a book or article and when you listen to tapes, have a note pad and pencil handy. Ideas are triggered when you study. Write them down as they come to you, otherwise, a good idea is often lost without a reminder note.

Accepting Responsibility

AFFIRMATION:
By the grace of God, I am in control of my life and my destiny. I have the strength and energy to do what I have to do and to be what I need to be. I live each day to the fullest. I am effective in all my dealings and I accept responsibility for my actions and, consequently, for my life.

TAKING CONTROL

YOUR LIFE AND YOUR FUTURE ARE IN YOUR CONTROL, DEPENDING ON HOW YOU REACT TO EVENTS THAT HAPPEN WHICH ARE BEYOND YOUR CONTROL. Isn't that exciting?

CONCENTRATE ON WHAT YOU CAN CONTROL.

PEOPLE: See the good in everyone. Expect the best. Do not try to change people to fit into your mold. Accept them as they are. Encourage them by setting an example they may want to follow. Enjoy the different personalities.

CONDITIONS: Most situations are not as bad as they seem. They have a way of working out when approached with the right attitude. Learn to look at problems as opportunities; know for every problem there is a solution. Remember, 90 percent of what you worry about never happens.

SURVEY THE CONDITION: What can you do to control it? If you find you can control the condition, do so quickly! If you find you cannot control the condition, keep moving. Many people get so "paralyzed" with a situation or condition beyond their control that they cannot function when they most need to work. If you can't control the condition, draw on your faith. Faith gives hope for good outcomes for conditions beyond your control.

SUGGESTED ACTIVITY:

Select six of the most difficult people you know. Approach them, offering your product, service or opportunity.

If they accept, they make the best customers and/or business associates.

If they reject, you are stronger and more knowledgeable because you have gained experience and understanding on dealing with difficult people.

Is there a condition or situation in your life that is holding you back? Ask yourself, "Can this situation be changed?" If yes, take steps to start changing it immediately. If not, don't give up, find another way.

Take responsibility for your life. You are in control when you accept the situations you can't change and change the ones you can. Self-control empowers you to achieve great success.

DEVELOPING OPTIMISM

What kind of person do you want to be? How do you want to be remembered? You have a choice! Optimism and pessimism are learned behavioral attitudes.

LEARN TO BE OPTIMISTIC. Optimists are achievers. They accomplish 80 percent of the work in 20 percent of the time. Pessimists accomplish 20 percent of the work in 80 percent of the time! Start at the beginning of the day. Now tell me, if you can learn to be an optimist, wouldn't you be interested in having more for less? Daytime is prime productive time if you are working with people. As you see results from your activity, you become more optimistic.

Learn to expect the most favorable acceptance of actions and events. Anticipate the best possible outcome.

This optimistic attitude acts as a magnet to attract whatever is needed to produce positive results.

People like to be around relaxed and friendly people. Associate with positive, happy people. If you find yourself in a crowd that is tense with dissatisfaction, fault-finding or griping, take charge! Change the subject to something positive, single out someone or something to praise. People will recognize you as an optimist and seek your company. They will buy what you sell, do as you say and refer you to others.

You can be too optimistic. Too much optimism can blind you to the truth. Couple optimism with activity and faith and you can overcome almost anything!

When tension or anxiety approach you, take a deep breath, breathe slowly, sit back and relax your muscles and respond calmly and positively to the problem. Say to yourself, "I am a believer. I can handle this situation."

 **SUGGESTED ACTIVITY:**

Set a recorder by your bed with a tape that plays good, positive music. As soon as you awaken, turn it on. As you listen to the upbeat music, thank God for a good day ahead.

Bounce out of bed. Look at yourself in the mirror. Say, "I feel great, I feel wonderful! I look great! Today is my best day ever!" Use any positive statement that gives you a feeling of getting started.

WAKE UP!

Read your positive affirmations for the day.

Read an inspirational message.

Refer to your activity list for the day and move ahead.

You will find the sun shines on you even in cloudy weather. Your optimistic attitude gives you enthusiasm that creates a magnet that attracts the best to you.

HANDLING STRESS

Everyone experiences stress to some degree. There is good stress and bad stress. Take heart, control and manage your stress with the right attitude.

Recognize some things that promote stress such as:

DISSATISFACTION WITH SELF, THE WAY YOU LOOK.

SOLUTION: Do not judge yourself on your shortcomings, but access your positive qualities. You have more good than bad. Make a list of your good qualities, concentrate on them. Many bad faults can be controlled. If you can correct your faults, make an effort to do so.

DISSATISFACTION WITH YOUR PERFORMANCE OR YOUR ACTIONS.

SOLUTION: Be grateful for the talent you have. Do not compare yourself to others. Think on the things you do well. Count your accomplishments and hold them in your mind. Read any positive notes you may have received from friends or associates. Pull back that "winning feeling" you experienced when you were pleased with yourself.

FEELING LACK IN YOUR LIFE.

SOLUTION: Count your blessings! You will find you have more abundance than lack in your life. **THINK ABUNDANCE!** In all things give thanks. Take steps to do whatever you can to learn, grow and change. What may appear as lack today will resurface as part of your growth program later in life if you do something now to correct the shortcoming of which you have become aware.

℞ SUGGESTED ACTIVITY:

To release stressful areas in your life, do a laughter exercise. Think of something that makes you laugh. Read a funny book, watch a funny show. It is scientifically proven that laughter reduces stress. Even forced laughter relaxes the stomach and throat muscles and gives a sense of well-being. Develop a sense of humor. You'll be healthier and attract happy people.

Talk about the thing that stresses you. Don't hold stressful thoughts and feelings inside. Once you talk it out, it does not seem nearly so serious. If you can't talk it out, write it out, then read what you have written and tear up the note. Throw it to the four winds! And laugh!

Get your body into action. Deep breathing exercises relieve stress. Get comfortable, take deep breaths, counting from ten to one, taking in and letting out. Feel your body relax. Activity is the best medicine for stress. Often stress is just an expression of self-pity and self-involvement. Action helps get your mind off yourself and is a wonderful cure. Anxiety causes stress while action reduces it! Do something—keep that circulation stirring.

Commit the stress to God. He will take it from you and free you to get on with your life. Trust gives faith and faith gives hope. It is difficult to be hopeful and stressed at the same time.

Recognize stress, but do not allow it to control you. Use it to your advantage as you follow these suggestions.

BE HAPPY

The pursuit of happiness is a futile quest, happiness never comes when it is the goal in life. It is, rather, a by-product of gracious living. No doubt the first step toward being happy is to acknowledge that you, and you alone, are responsible for your happiness! Doing the right thing, playing by the rules, honesty, decency and being other-people oriented, brings happiness. No one can steal your peace of mind, your sense of worth or your business opportunity unless you allow it. With positive thinking, success motivation and the willingness to be responsible for and to yourself, anything is possible and you will find that you are in control of your emotions. The results are a sense of well-being, peace and happiness.

BE MINDFUL OF YOUR APPEARANCE. Appear positive, prosperous, happy and satisfied. Appearances often dictate how others treat you as well as how you treat others. When you feel you are projecting your best, you have more confidence to reach out to others. They respond and happiness follows.

BREAK BAD HABITS. Recognize habits that hold you back and make a plan to free yourself of their mastery over you. Stop procrastinating. You know what you need to do each day for success. When you put off tasks and plans, you rob yourself of time, an unredeemable commodity. Guilt sets in, immobility and regret makes matters worse and wastes more time. Stick to your daily plan and get more out of each hour of the day. You will have a sense of well being for a productive day. You break habits one day at a time.

DEVELOP A SENSE OF VALUE TO THOSE WITH WHOM YOU ASSOCIATE. Be the person they can count on. Be knowledgeable about your business and be helpful to others in the business and in life. Feel that you are projecting an image that is important to your company's growth and to you as an individual.

BE INVOLVED. Become an "expert" in your field, and learn the little "extras" that make you important to your company and your customers. The more you know, the more valuable you are and the happier you become.

BECOME TOTALLY COMMITTED to doing what you know is right for you. Eliminate all activity that distracts from your positive image and your success. Be happy and grateful that you have ability and that you are making the most of it. Be the best you can be!

℞ SUGGESTED ACTIVITY:

Make a plan that you will use for the rest of your life.

Establish a daily routine for grooming. Never leave your house or answer your doorbell unless you look your very best and are dressed for the occasion. If you have an office in the home, dress for work each day. Be presentable, ready to meet the world.

Check your weekly plan and your daily plan. Set aside some time each day to study. Learn more about your business. Study your business guide. Study self-help books and programs. Do some serious reading daily. Your continued personal growth is essential.

Establish a schedule for activity. Do not allow postponements, cancellations and unexpected emergencies interfere with the business appointments to which you are committed.

These suggestions are examples of actions that make people happy and successful. You will find they will work for you and you will add to these suggestions as you continue to find ways and means to fulfill your goal to be a happy, successful person who attracts a following and makes a difference in the world.

Notes

Ethics

AFFIRMATION:
By the grace of God and with dedication and purpose, I reflect the highest professional standards of integrity, honesty and responsibility in dealings with my customers, business associates, my company and my peers.

CHARACTER

Never sacrifice your integrity on your way to the top. Your character is your most important asset. Guard it with your life! Live your life in such a way that you need never fear exposure and in such a way that you can look at yourself in the mirror with a clear conscience.

DO YOUR PART. Volunteer for extra tasks. The more you accept delegation, the better your chance for success.

KEEP YOUR PROMISES. Be responsible, do what you promise, even if you have to get help to do it. The person who gives the most gets the most in respect, admiration and education.

SERVE THE NEEDS OF OTHERS. Make it your specialty to service customer needs. Think about their wants. Give them hope. Show deep concern and consideration for them and help them to have your product by working with them. When you put your customer first, you will rise to the top.

BE TRUSTWORTHY. Make your deed as good as your word, and your word as good as your deed! Be the person people can trust and believe. Be honest and fair in all your dealings. Practicing the Golden Rule is putting yourself in the other person's shoes. If you are tempted to take another person's customer or potential business associate, ask yourself, "How would I feel if this happened to me?" Treat others as you want to be treated and you won't cheat and, chances are, you won't be cheated. But even if you are, your clear conscience gives happiness and success. Remember the law of return and realize if you sow good seed, good results will come. The reverse is also true. Attend to your business, keep your slate clean and let the other fellow do the same. Look for good in others. There is always something good about everyone. When you concentrate on good, you find it in the most unusual places.

BE DEPENDABLE. Be the person people can "count on" to follow through. Take care of your obligations in a consistent, pleasant manner. Pay your bills in a timely fashion. Good credit is valuable. Protect it.

PROTECT YOUR "COMPANY IMAGE." Keep in mind, everything one person does reflects on the entire group. Take responsibility for building a good, trustworthy image worthy of the company and the group you represent. This is a responsibility that comes with the opportunity you enjoy.

℞ SUGGESTED ACTIVITY:

Make a list of your good character traits. Recite this list daily. Make of list of character traits about which you are doubtful.

What can you do to correct this? Confidently set into action a plan to overcome these faults.

Keep track of your promises and commitments. Have you followed through?

Realize the commitments you make to yourself are more important than those you make to others. Be sure you follow through and be true to yourself.

COURTESY

If you want to make progress in your career, you will find it beneficial to regard the feelings of others at all times.

BE PUNCTUAL TO ALL MEETINGS AND APPOINTMENTS. Some people make a practice of being "fashionably late." There is no such thing. If you arrive at any meeting or appointment late, you are inconveniencing everyone there and showing lack of consideration. Being punctual is a reflection of good character. If for some reason you can't avoid being late, call and let the people who expect you know that you have been delayed.

ANSWER YOUR PHONE PROMPTLY. This shows respect for the caller. If you have call waiting, never keep the first caller on the line while talking to the second caller. Instead, tell the second caller you will call back or ask the second caller to hold while you release the first caller, and release quickly. Do not ask a person to hold while you look for information. Instead, ask if you may call back as soon as you have the information.

RETURN PHONE CALLS PROMPTLY. People judge your interest and credibility by your promptness. You know you like to have your calls returned promptly, show the same courtesy to others. It is good for business.

CONTROL PHONE TIME. Time is valuable to you and to the person with whom you are talking. Most calls can be handled in three minutes. After that, we start repeating ourselves. Keep an egg timer, a $10.00 bill and a book of matches by your phone. After three minutes light the match, after three and one-half minutes start burning the $10.00 bill. This will give you a sense of urgency to courteously end the conversation.

CONTROL THE URGE TO GOSSIP. Keep your mind and your conversation on pleasant, positive topics. If someone tells you something in confidence, hold that confidence and never let anyone know it was told to you, even if it later becomes public information. It is better to say, "I am unable to comment on that," than to get involved or take a chance of being misquoted. Never "take sides," avoid giving opinions or expressing your feelings in a conflict between other people. Listen, express your regret, be honestly empathetic or sympathetic. Refer business associates to professional counseling for personal problems. Confine your advice and guidance to business situations.

SUGGESTED ACTIVITY:

List all appointments for the week ahead. Keep track of your time of arrival. Were you on time? Were you late? How late?

Keep a log of your phone calls. Time yourself. See how many minutes you spent on each call. Write what you discussed and what you accomplished on each call. Did you burn any $10.00 bills? (Figuratively or actually?)

Be aware of courteous actions this week. Were you abrupt or considerate? Were you aware of better reception by others when you were courteous? Remember, be courteous to family members and loved ones, as well as customers and business associates!

COMPLAINTS

Anyone in business will hear some complaints. Complaints can be good because they call your attention to things or procedures that need to be corrected. If you are prepared to handle complaints and know how to graciously accept them, you will not dread complaints but you will learn from them.

Do not set your customer up to complain. When you deliver a product or service, never say, "If you have problems, call me." Rather, say, "If you have questions, call me." Do you see the difference? When you say "problem" you are setting your customer up for complaints on the product. When you say "question" you are letting your customer know you are knowledgeable about the product and available to help.

WHEN COMPLAINTS HAPPEN, HANDLE THEM. Never interrupt a complaining customer. Listen with interest, take notes if necessary. Get all the details you possibly can. If a complaint is made in person, look pleasant and be patient. Do not be on the defensive, do not argue with a customer and do not talk at all until the customer is finished with the complaint. Often, just talking it out will help the customer understand the problem. Once the customer is finished, do reassure that you will help. It is good to say, "I understand how you feel, and I will do all I can to help solve your problem." If you can't solve the problem yourself, tell the customer that you will speak with someone who can. Be clear, concise, honest and pleasant.

Give complainants a definite time when you will have an answer. Be sure to follow through and call back whether or not you have a solution just to let the person know you are still working on it. If someone else takes over the handling of the complaint, inform the customer, keeping the individual informed and apprised of your actions concerning the complaint until that person understands you are no longer handling the complaint.

If you have a company guarantee and the problem can be covered by your company guarantee, do so immediately in a courteous, friendly manner. If your guarantee offers refunds and the customer wants a refund and, if you sold the product, refund at once. If you did not sell the product and the customer wants a refund, make reference to the person from whom the product was purchased or to your company headquarters. If possible, exchange product the customer does not like for one that is usable and desirable.

The way you handle complaints speaks loud and clear. A complaint well- handled will gain respect and goodwill. Poorly handled complaints can be the worst possible advertisement. There is no end to how much damage an unsatisfied customer can do.

Your ethical standards and integrity are really on the line when it comes to complaints, so handle with care.

 **SUGGESTED ACTIVITY:**

Thoroughly study your company's product guarantee policy. Know proper procedure for honoring the guarantee. Be prepared to follow it to the letter, no exceptions. Proper handling will build goodwill for you and your company.

Study the section in your business guide concerning your company's history, philosophy, code of ethics and image. Study the section in your business guide regarding career guidelines. Be prepared to answer questions on these subjects any time.

THE GOLDEN RULE

So often we quote the Golden Rule, but do we really grasp the true meaning of what we are saying? Do we really practice and live by the Golden Rule? These questions inspired this writing.

Let us admonish ourselves to embrace the spirit of this law and not just the words. What is the real reason we should do unto others as we'd have them to do unto us if the condition were reversed?

You may elect to deal unjustly with others, but according to God's word, "Whatsoever a man soweth that shall he also reap." This unjustness will come back to you. The same rule applies when you deal justly with others. Good will come back to you. Keep in mind this law is not limited by your actions but also by your thoughts. We are the sum total of our thoughts: "As a man thinketh in his heart, so is he." Our thoughts and our actions are what take us to the heights of success and happiness or to the pits of failure and despair. Success meaning not only financial and physical success, but inner peace, happiness and freedom gained through spreading peace, happiness and freedom to others unselfishly.

Our concern should not be so much that we are not cheated, but rather that we cheat not. Then we will find all things do work together for our good, and we find joy, success and happiness in our lives and business. Financial success at the cost or loss of happiness is failure. Let's say we are cheated. Someone takes a prospective customer or business associate on whom we were counting. The deal is final; the case is closed. What shall we do?

This is where prayer helps us practice the Golden Rule.

Petition the situation to God and admit we feel we've been wronged.

Confess we do not know the mind of God, and that we trust Him to do the right thing for the benefit of all concerned.

Release what we thought was ours; ask God's blessings.

Pray for the person we feel cheated us.

Thank the Lord for past and future blessings and get on with our lives.

Granted, this is not easy to do, but it is the thing to do if we want happiness and success. This is what it means to practice the Golden Rule. We can be strengthened by injustice so long as we accept it, release it, bless it and move on.

Our attitude greatly influences our lives and is a secret power working 24 hours a day for good or bad. It is important to be in control. Through prayer we have control so that we do not blatantly cheat others.

Your character will publish itself. You cannot appear to practice the Golden Rule and at heart misuse this universal law for selfish and covetous gain. Eventually what you are, good or bad, will reflect in your face, your attitude and your life.

Control your thoughts. Think for your good and gain in relation to the good and gain you give to others, and you have begun to capture the essence of the Golden Rule. Our world is a mirror or "looking glass." It reflects our attitudes, actions and words. Give out good, and good is reflected. If you're having a "bad day," check your attitude and pray. Thank God for the day and commit it to Him—and notice how everyone and everything changes because you have changed!

SUGGESTED ACTIVITY:

Make this your motto:
To have respect — Give respect.
To have trust — Give trust.
To have love — Give love.
What you give returns to you in forms you may not recognize, but it does return.

Notes

Confidence Builders

AFFIRMATION:
I have the faith and belief that I will act in a right, proper and effective way. I am able to rely on my own convictions. I am at ease with all situations because I have faith, knowledge, love and assurance. I continue to grow in confidence with constant learning and understanding of myself, others and each situation I face in my personal life and on my job.

FORGIVENESS AND APPRECIATION

A happy countenance is the result of a mind at peace with itself and others. To have freedom, happiness, satisfaction and confidence, you will find a wonderful secret in the art of appreciation. Giving thanks for all things makes each burden a blessing and a growth experience for you. Forgiveness becomes second nature because you are aware that, with a grateful spirit, you can handle whatever hurt or slight may come your way. Sometimes you do not even notice the slights!

Holding grudges against yourself and others destroys your confidence. As you begin your journey into building or rebuilding self-confidence, think of all the hurts, insults, slights, real or imaginary, you have felt and held in your memory. Because you are building a new image of yourself, it is necessary to rid your mind of these negative influences, flush them out and start over.

As a confident individual you will feel too big, too self-reliant to be threatened. You will be able to forgive others for hurts and injustices with no strings attached. Once you release these feelings through forgiveness, you are free to grow and appreciate all the good and all the bad in your life. You are ridding yourself of negative thoughts and you are capitalizing on positive thoughts.

Practice forgiving yourself for past mistakes and inadequacies. Be thankful for the abilities and the attributes you have. Once you face up to your shortcomings and your feelings of guilt, you are, with God's help, able to forgive yourself. You can then replace these inadequacies with positive thoughts and actions, and gain acceptance for yourself.

Realize the past is gone. Yes, it is an influence on your life, but negative experiences of the past need not control your life, and they won't, if you face them, forgive yourself and make changes. This will free you to concentrate on past successes and past actions, feel good about yourself and benefit from them, as you live for today and project your future.

Pull on the past through forgiveness of your personal faults and faults of others, through praise and appreciation for personal victories and for positive contributions others have made in your life. When you do this, you benefit from the past, giving you a great today and help to plan for a self-confident, satisfying future.

You will find you need to practice this "cleansing" daily. At the beginning of each day you will look forward to positive activities with thanksgiving and hope. At the end of each day you will close with forgiveness and appreciation. Your confidence will grow day by day.

℞ SUGGESTED ACTIVITY:

Make a list of past mistakes, hurts and enemies. For each one write a note of forgiveness. If it is possible, you may want to contact the individual you are forgiving in person. If that is not possible, just feel the forgiveness and ask the Lord's blessing on that individual.

Do the same for yourself. Acknowledge what you don't like about yourself and write yourself a note of forgiveness.

Write a list of all past grudges and prejudices you have held. Thank God for cleansing your heart of these feelings. Tear this list in a million pieces. Toss it to the four winds and say to yourself, "They are no more."

Now that you've "covered" the past, make this a daily practice.

WHO ARE YOU

How do you see yourself? You have within you a force for success, happiness and satisfaction, among other attributes. This force for success gives you a sense of direction, courage, compassion and self-respect.

Some enemies of your force for success are frustration, resentment, hurt feelings, loneliness, emptiness, and these are just a few. You can surely add more to the list, if you are of the nature to do so.

The choice is yours. In this journey we call life, we encounter people and experiences that will build us up and some that will tear us down, but we have a choice to cancel the obstacles that rob us of our self-confidence and self-image.

Through creative thinking, it is possible to turn every negative influence into positive and to build your self-image by facing the fear, overcoming the frustration through activity, smiling and being grateful through hurt feelings and loneliness.

Everyone has some successful, happy times. Possibly very minimal, but we all have some memory or memories in our life that we can think back to and gain the confidence to get us through a present adversity or feeling of inadequacy. Every time we practice this, our self-image and our ability grows stronger. Dwell on the negative and lose your confidence; concentrate on the positive and build your confidence. Indeed, in the throes of trouble and heartbreak this is not easy, but it is necessary and you grow and become stronger for having experienced and overcome the affliction.

You will find you are replacing old recordings of past blunders as you concentrate on past victories.

Are you facing a task or situation that is frightening to you? Maybe your self-confidence is threatened because you feel you are not "up to" doing a good job.

Stop and think about your past victories! Yes, you have some, regardless how small or how long ago. Pull on that winning feeling. Black out all drawbacks. Stand straight, face the task with confidence, go out and do the job. You will find you feel great! You did it! Chalk it up to one more victory you can recall when your self-image and self-confidence needs a boost.

You are on your way! You are a worthwhile, happy human being necessary to make this universe what it is today. Never underestimate the importance of acknowledging that you do play an important part in this world or you would not be here. As you continue to grow and discover and get to know who you are, you will find your place in the sun and you will make a difference for having lived.

SUGGESTED ACTIVITY:

Make a list of past victories that made you feel like a winner.

Go back to your first memories and include every instance, every person that made you feel good about yourself.

Prepare this list in big letters. When your self-image needs a boost, read your list.

Perform a business task that you feel a little uncomfortable doing. Do this task six different times. Each time you complete this task, make a written summary of your feelings and growth.

PEACE OF MIND

To be calm in the storm, to keep moving ahead against the wind, to hold your head high, keep your body agile, you will need a great deal of self-control and a delicate balance between mind and body. To have peace of mind and build confidence, you must grow in areas such as:

POISE

Developing knowledge and ability to handle fundamentals, to be prepared, to plan and execute action, gives you the freedom to be yourself and to feel at ease in any situation. This is accomplished through dedicated study and putting into practice what you have learned by actually doing the work to accomplish worthwhile achievements.

ENTHUSIASM

There is no substitute for this very important trait that insures peace of mind and confidence. Put your heart into your work. Take joy in exhilarating others. Have team spirit and don't be concerned about getting the credit so long as the plan works. Your reward comes from respect without fear, from faith in yourself and the ability to stay on course. This generates enthusiasm and you develop an aura that attracts others. The more your attract, the more enthusiastic you become.

LOYALTY

Be loyal to yourself and all who depend on you, your company, your leaders and your followers. Cooperate with all levels. Build mutual esteem, respect and devotion, and be totally sincere and honest with nothing to hide.

INDUSTRIOUSNESS

Desire to excel in your life, in your work and in your plan. Focus your ambition and cultivate the ability to make decisions, and to think for yourself. Be the best at what you do in your spiritual, personal, family and business life.

℞ SUGGESTED ACTIVITY:

Review poise, enthusiasm, loyalty and industriousness. Grade yourself. How do you measure up?

Get serious about your present and future life. Set priorities. Find out what is important to you and give that aspect the priority it deserves.

Peace of mind comes from satisfaction of knowing you did your best to become the best.

THE REWARDS

As you become aware and focus on confidence builders, you will find your self-confidence increases.

Self-confidence is gained through knowledge, experience and in practicing the suggestions in this chapter. You will have gained much because of your willingness to perform the exercises, to do the work, to study and to have done the things you have feared. These ideas will open your mind to other suggestions and avenues that will continue to give you the ability to overcome obstacles and situations and help you to become a strong individual who can help others to happiness and growth. When you do this, you have experienced true growth.

As you deal honestly with your shortcomings and as you become consistent in your growth and your ability to correct your errors, you gain a healthy respect for yourself which enhances your self-esteem and gives you courage to keep charging ahead to success and satisfaction.

Your new found self-confidence gives you the power to have clear vision concerning your desire for what you really want to achieve in life. You will be able to focus clearly on your goals for achievement, personal success and happiness with strong emotion that overcomes obstacles successfully.

You will delight in action, having the confidence to follow a plan of action that requires a little more of you than ever before and perhaps a little more than you feel you can achieve. As you taste the victory of each activity for which you have stretched, you gain added confidence to try a little more. This gives you tremendous self-motivation and you experience the joy of playing the game of "self-competition"—beating your best record. **Amateurs compete with other people. Professionals compete with themselves.** You are a "pro" in all areas of your life.

Becoming the example to yourself through confidence gained by performance puts you in position to become the example to others and enables you to help them reach the joy you have achieved as a self-confident individual. You will find confidence continually reinforces your ability through continuous experience, doubles your energy through enthusiasm for having achieved, expands your mental faculties through desire for study and increases your personal power through application of what you have learned.

 SUGGESTED ACTIVITY:

Review your goal plan. Does it complement your new-found confidence? If not, set your goals to bring them up to your present feelings and desires in all areas of your life—spiritual, personal, family, business. Keep in mind your goals change as your level of understanding increases.

Review your plan of action. Set your plan so that, daily, you stretch to achieve your goal. Each day, plan to do a little more than you did the day before. You're sure to get more accomplished for having made a plan than you would have with no plan.

It's admirable and advantageous to set your plan of action for a little more than you really believe you can accomplish, then stretch to accomplish or exceed.

Share your plan with another person and help that person make a plan for achievement with your guidance. As a responsible person to someone else, you are encouraged to stay with the plan you have made and are sharing.

Notes

℞

Happiness Through Significance

AFFIRMATION:
By the grace of God, I feel significant because I am making a difference in this world. My desire is to help others feel significant and to fill their needs. I know I can achieve this through my actions, words and deeds as I contribute something of value to everyone I meet.

SIGNIFICANCE THROUGH WORK

Why do we work? On one level, we work to pay the bills, to survive. But the deeper reason we work is to obtain our goals and objectives, to satisfy our intense desire to be something—to be significant in our own eyes and in the eyes of those we love.

How much money we earn is a small part of feeling significant. We feel significant by overcoming life's hurdles and defeats. By doing the right thing, playing by the rules, the money follows.

Strive to be exceptional. Don't be satisfied with doing an average day's work. Very few people operate at their highest level. Once you zero in on what you want to achieve, make a pact with yourself to give it all you've got, to be exceptional, to perform at the maximum. Work with intensity. Fall in love with what you will be doing and you will never tire of the task. It will become a joy and a way of life for you.

Integrity is a great part of feeling significant, never compromising your ideals. Be dedicated to helping others. Take delight in extending yourself and your abilities to help others. Concentrate on other people's needs and your own will be met in a very beautiful way. Serving the needs of others is a big part of feeling significant. If you can make a difference in someone's life, you have contributed to that individual and to the world in general. There are many ways to serve the needs of others and be handsomely paid for it both in money and significance.

The joy of service makes work pleasurable and it becomes a mission which sparks an intense desire to accomplish objectives. Our guidance system takes over and new ideas and inspiration, as well as enthusiasm and energy, flow into our thoughts and experience in the form of creative thoughts or hunches that help us reach our goal.

SUGGESTED ACTIVITY:

Set five to 15 appointments and make your presentation with the main objective to meet the needs of others. Forgetting what you get from these appointments, think of "**giving**" and feeling significant by sharing.

After each appointment, evaluate the difference in the attitude of the people you are serving as well as your feeling of success. Check the dollar value of these appointments. Was it higher than usual?

WHAT'S THE POINT

Everyone wants to be significant! This feeling seems to be a "built in" survival system in each of us!

It is a normal human desire to want to "make a difference" in this world, to make our lives "count." In order to make a contribution, it is necessary to accept responsibility to prepare yourself in a field of endeavor or service which enables you to reach out, to help, encourage, teach, and, in general, make a contribution to human kind.

A great part of making yourself feel significant is making others feel significant. Showing interest, concern, appreciation and recognition to others reflects back to you in their response.

In order to make a contribution, it is necessary to accept responsibility. Empowerment to assume responsibility and make a difference involves many factors.

FAITH. Have faith in God and in yourself to do the right thing. Be dedicated to your spiritual beliefs. Have fellowship with others of like faith and, daily, pray and study for guidance, knowledge and inspiration.

HEALTH. Strength to persevere in the face of obstacles, drawbacks, difficulties and disappointments is essential. Follow a good nutrition program and get plenty of exercise. Keep a health check with regular physicals and curb habits which inhibit good health.

ATTITUDE. Keep a positive, happy outlook. Negativity blocks the ability to achieve, grow and serve. Optimism can be developed, even by pessimistic people. It takes continual application, dedication and practice. Seek out optimists and stay away from pessimists.

℞ SUGGESTED ACTIVITY:

Never stop learning. Make an outline for a study guide that will give you more comprehensive knowledge of your field of endeavor, using your career guide, books and tapes. Plan to study a minimum of one hour each day.

Make a commitment to get in control of your life by taking steps to overcome habits that may be controlling you.

Make an appointment for a health check. It is possible to be so dedicated to everything and everyone else that you neglect your own health. The price is too high, don't do this!

Make a written list of positive attitude qualities you already possess. Make a list of bad attitudes, fears, inhibitions you may have. Work out a plan of action to correct these by spending time reading positive affirmations, associating with positive people, etc.

SIGNIFICANCE THROUGH COURAGE

Recognize the difference between failure and temporary defeat.

Every person of significance has experienced temporary defeat and has found it made them stronger and more capable. We are in constant preparation for success and significance. Give thanks for the defeats and they become blessings.

Have the courage to press on with a positive attitude and action during adversity.

BE PREPARED FOR SETBACKS.

Do not fear setbacks or expect them, but be prepared. When you are prepared, you will avoid being unable to act and prevent having your self-esteem undermined.

A very successful man I know once told me for every success plan he had an alternate plan. That way if something happened to "Plan A" he could go right to "Plan B." (Incidently, that is one reason I married him.)

I used to work by appointment. Of course, I expected the appointments to hold and they usually did, but I was prepared for possible postponements by scheduling more appointments closer together than I really wanted to hold. If I had no appointment scheduled, to offset a postponement, I had a prospect list to call, using the postponed appointment time to make contacts and new appointments. I found this alternative very helpful and never felt "down" because of postponements. Sometimes, I even welcomed them.

CAPITALIZE ON YOUR ABILITY TO MAKE A NEW START. You are resilient. Believe you are capable of withstanding the shock of loss without permanent damage and you will regroup and come back stronger than before! Never give up! If one approach does not work, seek out another. Often, the second (or even the 15th) attempt is the one that brings about the greatest significance.

℞ SUGGESTED ACTIVITY:

Write your "success plan." Now, figure out an alternate plan. Give the original plan your complete focus, but be prepared to switch gears if need be.

Review your appointments for the week. Double up.

Check your "prospect list." Update and increase it and keep it current. Be prepared to work this list in case of postponements.

SIGNIFICANCE THROUGH ACTION

Your significance will be discovered and acknowledged by others as a result of your actions. The best sales presentation you can make for yourself is achieved by demonstrating your abilities, rather than talking about them.

Act on your dreams! The turtle does not travel until he sticks his neck out. When you are inclined to hesitate, think of the turtle. Stick your neck out and go for your dream! Dreams are great but without action they are wasted energy!

Others make you feel significant. Never get so busy or so important that you do not have time for others. Make a pact with yourself to do a good deed every day. Good deeds may be large or small, it matters not. Just a smile or a "thank you" can mean a lot to some people, and when you give out you become significant in their eyes. This is significance that counts and puts you in position to make your dreams come true.

Accept the fact that everyone may not like you or, possibly, you may be misunderstood. In this case, rather than words, show consistent action. Go about your business and demonstrate that you are a kind, caring and generous individual, and, at the same time, that you are strong and fair. People often judge you by your deeds, not your words.

Consistent action, continually developing a following, always building your business will set in motion a force for good that will remain long after you are gone. How do you want to be remembered? Positive action touches lives and brings results which will leave your mark on the world.

Be passionate about your work. Do your job to the glory of God and you will attract the admiration of people and have success far beyond your normal expectations. Take joy in showing your product or performing your service and you will earn a reputation of responsibility and dependability as a staunch, trustworthy business person. You will have the respect and admiration of all who know you. This is significance!

Be remembered as a person who set an example for others to follow. Be remembered as a trail blazer and one who made a difference in the lives of others. This is true significance.

SUGGESTED ACTIVITY:

Each day, dedicate yourself to simple acts of kindness. Just small things you can do for others. Soon you will find you are doing these things and not even thinking about them. They just happen because you have entrenched them as part of your personality.

Make others feel significant and they will return the gesture to you!

℞

You Can Do It

AFFIRMATION:
Yes, I can do it! I am aware that I will not desire anything I am not capable of achieving. It is just a matter of time, faith, information and physical application. My desire will give me the strength and energy to be what I need to be and to do what I have to do!

GET SERIOUS

Life is a promise and a threat. Start building and accepting promise right now and you need never feel threatened.

DECIDE WHAT YOU WANT FROM LIFE! Have a definite plan and give yourself no way out. When you are in a no-way-out situation, you will defend your goals, your plan of action and your desires with all your heart.

TO BUILD AND DEFEND YOU MUST BE TOTALLY COMMITTED.

SUCCESS IN BUSINESS GIVES YOU SECURITY AND FREEDOM TO ENJOY EVERY FACET OF YOUR LIFE. Being totally committed does not mean you have to be working at the job 24 hours a day. It means you must determine when and how much you need to work to accomplish your goal, and then let nothing deter you from that plan.

WHAT DOES YOUR JOB REQUIRE FOR SUCCESS? Find the answer to this question and write it down. When you write, you crystalize your thinking and your written statement becomes tangible. You can grasp it. Until you write a job description and job requirement, you do not have a firm understanding and you cannot make a definite commitment.

Once you have written your job description and your job requirement, investigate and see what is required of you to meet these specifications.

When you have a clear picture of what you want and what is required to achieve your desire, you are ready to set your goals for accomplishment and make a plan of action. You have a mind set, a confidence and desire that will keep you forging ahead.

SUGGESTED ACTIVITY:

Research your job and its requirements. Write this in clear, concise form in your own handwriting.

Review your goals and plan of action. If you have not formatted this, do it now, using job requirements as a guide to establish these goals and plan of action.

Study everything you can pertaining to job requirements and rewards. This will give you emotional support and keep you going in the weeks and months to come.

GET SMART

People who work smart accomplish more in less time than those who work hard. Search for ideas. You have some magnificent sources.

YOUR OWN EXPERIENCE. If you are doing things wrong, find out why and change. You can change the way you are, if the way you are is not accomplishing what you want. Analyze your modus operandi and see if it is working. Add to, take from, and do what is necessary to make it work.

Do not underestimate a program of activity that has worked for you in the past. Often, we are so eager to put every "new idea" into practice, we pursue a course that may not be the answer. Be open to new ideas and be willing to make changes, but do it with a certain amount of reservation and see if it works for you before making a total change.

LEARN FROM OTHER PEOPLE. In our country we have a host of successful people who have implemented certain policies and ideas that have become standard. Look to the people who have done what you are doing now, and to people who have had satisfactory outcomes from their activities.

FIND A ROLE MODEL. Ask questions and follow the lead and example that your role model shares.

READ BOOKS. We are living in an age that affords us multitudes of good books to assist us in developing attitude, understanding, inspiration and motivation. Also, most companies have a business guide. Read this business guide to acquaint yourself with your particular company. This guide is usually assembled from experience of others who have gone before you and is written to help you become an expert in your field of endeavor.

LISTEN TO AUDIO TAPES. Listening to tapes while you are engaged in a conscious task such as driving, riding, getting ready for work, walking, etc., can be very effective. The message on the tape seems to sink into your subconscious (or creative) mind when your conscious mind is engaged in another task. You will be amazed by how much will retain and remember when playing a tape in this manner. It is a good idea to listen to the same tape three to six times before going on to another one.

UTILIZE PUBLICATIONS. If your company has a weekly or monthly publication, as you read it, cut out helpful ideas that you will use in your business. Make files on subject matter and file alphabetically for quick reference. Do the same thing when you are reading magazines, trade journals or any publication that is of interest to you.

SUGGESTED ACTIVITY:

Put all of the above ideas into practice. Tabulate your progress and what you have learned.

As a defender, you will do what it takes!

GET GOING AND GET EXCITED

Perhaps procrastination and hesitation hold more people back than anything else. Many people who have ability, aptitude and ambition allow fear of a bad outcome to keep them from getting started on a job, mission or project.

If you are dedicated to be a defender of your goals, you cannot afford to allow this to happen to you. Action is required!

DO SOMETHING! Even if you do not have the right procedure or it does not work, **you must start somewhere**. You learn from your mistakes. Thinking about action exhausts you; motion renews your strength and creates more motion in the right direction. You will **not** continue going the wrong way on a one way street. Mere force will turn you the right direction, but you have to get started to find out which way to go!

BE FLEXIBLE. Perfectionists wait forever to know enough, for the right time and hold back for fear they will not live up to their own standards. Rigid perfectionists never accomplish much. Remember, you must be flexible or you may get "bent out of shape!"

ALWAYS HAVE AN ALTERNATE PLAN. If Plan A is not working, then go to Plan B. With alternate plans and alternate approaches, you are not so fenced in with your work. This makes you more effective.

MAKE EACH DAY COUNT. Your daily activity is critical to reaching your long- term goal. You do not and cannot control time, but you can control activities. Learn to live in day-tight compartments and get the most of each day. Every day is aflame with energy, opportunity and the presence of God. Every golden hour is a tiny square in the mosaic of God's beautiful plan for your life.

GET EXCITED. Visualization of having done what you are thinking about will get you excited. Feel the thrill of praise, hear the roar of the crowd. It will put a twinkle in your eye and a smile on your face that will give you a magnetism that will attract others to you. Eventually you bring about, to some degree, that which you visualize.

DRESS THE PART. Look and act like the person you want to become. Feel like every person you meet is potentially responsible for your success and that you must make a good impression. You will!

SUGGESTED ACTIVITY:

Put your technical knowledge to work. Arrange appointments to see the maximum amount of people and acquaint them with your product, service or opportunity.

Record your success, the way you feel about your progress and the excitement you feel about your career.

SUMMARY AND REVIEW

Keep in mind, you have four major areas in your life: Spiritual, personal, family and career. It is important for your success and well-being that you have some balance between these four areas. Neglecting one will affect the other. Your life will be out of balance and this will reflect in your personality (mentally, physically and emotionally).

Plan spiritual, personal and family time just as carefully as you plan your career time. As you prepare your ideal plan for the week, include all these areas and set aside definite times for each one. You will never stay totally within your ideal plan, but if you have scheduled the activity and the time required, you will, more than likely, make the time for this balance.

SPIRITUAL TIME spent gives you added strength, faith, inspiration and hope. This gives you divine help and power and adds to your life in general. It is the most important aspect of creating a balanced, effective life.

PERSONAL TIME is vital. You cannot keep the pace and handle everything you desire if you do not take time for personal care, activities, friendships and rest. I recommend a 15 minute "power nap" every afternoon, if you can fit it in. This is productive time and gives you power to finish the day and put in longer hours. In order for this to be a "power nap," you must not rest more than 15 minutes.

FAMILY TIME is essential to your happiness and productivity. You can reach tremendous success in business, but if you lose your family or fail your responsibility as a spouse or parent, you are a failure. Nothing is worth neglecting those you love the most. You need not neglect any of your four priorities. With proper planning and communications you can have it all. Share plans and goals with your family and solicit their help, understanding and support. Make family plans for the business and set aside quality, enjoyable time to spend with them apart from business. Reward yourself and your family after a successful business deal with some special time.

CAREER TIME is essential to your success and well-being. When you have taken care of the other three aspects of your life, you will find your work a wonderful, enjoyable release. You will be more effective and more productive because you won't be over balanced with work. Everyone seems to get "fed up" with work at some time or another. When this happens, mentally quit for an hour, a day or maybe two days (no longer). As you quit, take from yourself all the assets your career offers and see how you would feel without it. Chances are you will "start again" very quickly with renewed dedication, determination, appreciation and respect for what you have.

YOUR ENTIRE LIFE interacts and you are a believer, an individual, part of a family and a career person 24 hours a day. Each part makes up the whole of what you are. Planning will insure that you do all parts well.

LIFE IS A JOURNEY, A PROMISE AND A THREAT. Handle yours wisely and you will enjoy the trip and leave your mark on the world.

Notes

Luella Gunter

Luella Gunter is an example of a self-made, self-educated, successful woman. She finished high school just as she turned 18, and went to work for a criminal defense attorney. She completed a correspondence course and, through study and experience, became a successful legal secretary. Feeling the need to move ahead, Luella went to work for a certified public accountant, attended accounting classes at night and became a successful accountant. She eventually elevated to private accounting and office manager. Desiring a business of her own, an unexpected introduction to Mary Kay, Inc. peaked her interest and intrigue in the cosmetic business. She became an independent beauty consultant, representing that organization in 1966, when the company was two and one-half years old. Being the only consultant in Albuquerque, New Mexico, at the time, she learned the business by reading the consultant's guide and from experience. Through her diligence, she promoted herself to the highest position available in the company, that of Senior National Sales Director Emeritus, Mary Kay, Inc. Not one to rest on her laurels, Luella spends her time writing and as a guest speaker for various organizations, worldwide, sharing her experience and knowledge which she has gleaned through the years with others, and feels one must never stop growing. She says you are never too rich, too poor, too young or too old to learn something new. Certainly she keeps her mind keen with her various activities and many friends and acquaintances. She and her husband, Pres, enjoy each other and their many ventures and adventures.

Luella gives credit for a lot of her success to the study of the Holy Bible, especially the Book of Proverbs, as a child growing up, and to such great writers as Dale Carnegie and Benjamin Franklin as she was starting her self-education and, later, to such writers and speakers as Norman Vincent Peale, Zig Ziglar, Cavett Robert and many others. She has a strong faith in God and she says she seldom makes a decision without consulting God in prayer and discussing it with her husband.

Luella has made several tapes and videos available, which are listed on the order blank in this book.

If you or your group would like to have Luella visit you as a guest speaker for your functions such as meetings, retreats or workshops, you may reach her at Lupresco, Inc., (505) 822-0706.

Notes

Notes

Notes

Luella has made available the following tapes:

The Art of Persuasion & Visual Communication

An adventure into understanding people. This tape teaches you how to read body language, body build, facial expression and effective communication.

Self-Motivation

This tape teaches you how to take charge of your life and go to the top with self-motivation and attitude control.

Handling Frustration and Developing Persistence

This is a tape of the video, Handling Frustration and Developing Persistence.

Goals

This tape is full of fun and information and you get the whole process of goal setting, follow through and theory of setting goals. Can be adapted to any business.

Luella has also made two video tapes:

Handling Frustration and Developing Persistence

This tape handles everything from attitude, to goal setting, plan of action and persistence. Can be adapted to any business.

My Story — Luella Gunter

This video will give you hope! This is an overview of Luella's career with Mary Kay, Inc., however, anyone in direct sales will find it beneficial. Informative and fun to watch.

ALL THESE TAPES HAVE BEEN APPROVED BY MARY KAY, INC.

ORDER BLANK

MAIL TO: Lupresco, Inc. (505) 822-0706
5902 Torreon NE
Albuquerque, NM 87109

		QTY	TOTAL
Handling Frustration & Developing Persistence	$19.95	_____	__________
My Story — Luella Gunter	$19.95	_____	__________
The Art of Persuasion & Visual Comunication	$ 5.00	_____	__________
Self-Motivation	$ 5.00	_____	__________
Handling Frustration & Developing Persistence	$ 5.00	_____	__________
Goals	$ 5.00	_____	__________
Shipping and Handling	$ 3.00		__________
TOTAL ORDER			__________

Check Tapes Wanted, Total Order, and Method of Payment

Check ___ Credit Card ____ Expiration Date __________

Mastercard/Visa No. ______________________________

Name ______________________________________

Address ____________________________________

____

Telephone __________________________________